The Visual Manager

Copyright © 2015 Jon Moreton
The right of Jon Moreton to be identified as the author of this work has been asserted by him in accordance with the Copyright, Designs and Patents Act 1988.
All rights reserved.

ISBN 978-1-326-47068-5

DEDICATION

This book is dedicated to all managers active in an operational environment. It's a tough place to be in; but it can be a great place when teamwork starts to deliver results.

ACKNOWLEDGEMENTS

I'd like to thank ...

My wife, Magda, for her love and support. Without her, I could not have seen this through.

Francesca Bednarova-Harrison for her valuable advice.

My editor, Julie Lewthwaite, for her great support and advice, and for keeping me moving forward.

My friend and fellow consultant, Mark Mayer, for his kind permission to include visual content that he created.

All my friends and colleagues from RWD, my customers, and everyone I have worked with in the pursuit of operational improvement.

The Visual Manager

Jon Moreton

Contents

Foreword 5

Why I wrote this book 7

About the book 9

How to use this book 11

Chapter 1: Change, and a challenge 13

Chapter 2: Reflection and resolve 19

Chapter 3: Visual management basics explained 23

Chapter 4: First steps in visual management 45

Chapter 5: Paul under pressure 55

Chapter 6: Visual management process confirmation 57

Chapter 7: Getting the team on board 71

Chapter 8: Meeting mayhem 87

Chapter 9: Mike's formula for effective VM review meetings 89

Chapter 10: Solid progress – and a further challenge 105

Chapter 11: Getting results with visual management 117

Chapter 12: Looking to the future 133

Appendices 137

About the author 153

Foreword

Some businesses are successful despite themselves. Most survive and thrive because they understand the interdependencies within their teams and the critical nature of having real time information that is visible to track performance. This enables management to identify early problems and potential solutions to get back on track and to continually improve their operations. Too often problems are not tackled when they first occur due to a lack of information or because Managers have a habit of telling you what they think you want to hear, however well-intentioned they may be. Ultimately, responsibility rests with you.

Process improvement and lean thinking does not have to be complicated. This book describes simple methods for creating high visibility of results and progress in the workplace. By using visual management to drive the right behaviour, any business can be better organised and improve their results.

I enjoyed reading this book as it deals with the topic in a straight forward manner, presenting as it does a simple and complete system for operational improvement. It is designed for anyone who is interested in continually improving their own performance and the business within which they work.

Graham Rusling

Chairman of Evolute 360 Consulting Limited
(former Global Head of Business Support, Barclays)

JON MORETON

Why I wrote this book

There's a need for more simple, practical solutions to help managers improve their operations and get better results by working more closely with their teams. I think we need more books on the real, practical application of improvement techniques. When I was a manager, in a fast-moving operational environment, all I wanted to read were simple books that gave me practical ideas which I could go and implement to get results.

This book is for operations directors, operations managers, managing directors and all levels of management focused on day-to-day delivery of results.

I've been involved in the application of performance improvement methods, including Lean & and Six Sigma, for the past 20 years. I've worked both as a manager on the receiving end of performance improvement programmes, and as a consultant driving these programmes.

Gradually, over the years, I've realised that as sorely as people need to understand the tools of operational performance improvement, they need still more understanding of the conduct and attitudes necessary to make these tools work.

Of all the ideas currently developed to drive organisational performance improvement, I've found visual management to be one of the most powerful.

Visual management is a simple, practical technique with a direct focus on results. It simplifies the complexities of the operational environment and focuses people on the vital few problems that need to be solved. It reveals interdependencies between departments and can be adapted to suit any type of organisation, regardless of industry type.

This is not a book about the theory of visual management. This is a book based on the real experience of implementing visual management.

JON MORETON

About the book

You're about to read the story of Paul Wayman, an experienced manager whom I've invented. Paul is abruptly displaced from his comfort zone when the organisation he works for is the subject of a takeover. He's forced to adapt swiftly in order to survive.

As Paul learns new skills and techniques and meets with both successes and setbacks, so you, the reader, can learn from his experiences – and hopefully avoid making some of his mistakes.

While Paul's story is fictionalised, the lessons from it are hard fact. They're based on the author's years of management experience and learning, and are intended to help you to be more successful in your career.

JON MORETON

How to use this book

This book is intended to be a practical resource, not something interesting you read and then put back on the shelf and forget about. I want it to change things – the way you work, the way you think, the results you achieve.

I encourage you to make notes in the margin, underline or highlight words and passages, dog-ear the pages and do whatever is necessary for you to gain maximum benefit from it.

For brevity's sake, I haven't explained each of the management concepts I refer to. However, I also don't want to baffle anyone, so instead I've included appendices with overviews and relevant graphics, and included references in the text to guide you to the information.

JON MORETON

Chapter 1

Change, and a challenge

Paul Wayman drove through the entrance gates and pulled into a parking space outside his office at 7.25 a.m. Even taking into account the early morning management meeting he was there to attend, the car park was unusually full and there were a number of cars he didn't recognise – a bright red Mercedes, an overly large BMW, a black Range Rover, all with private number plates. They gleamed in the early morning sun. Feeling suddenly anxious, he grabbed his satchel and hurried towards the building.

Paul turned on his mobile phone as he pushed the front door open and was surprised to see he'd already missed three calls. The reception area was eerily empty, making him even more certain that something was going on. He trotted towards the glass walled boardroom and saw a tall man in a dark suit – not someone he recognised – presenting to a standing-room-only audience. It looked like the entire senior management team was there, as well as the board members themselves, plus maybe half a dozen strangers. He sneaked in at the back just as the speaker started to wrap up his presentation. He might have missed the meat of the speech, but Paul was in time for the only words he needed to hear to put him fully in the picture.

'So, in summary, this company has been subject to a takeover and we are the new owners.' The man straightened up his papers. 'We'll be speaking to each of you in due course, and making a statement to all employees and the press. Thank you.'

He walked out and his colleagues followed him, leaving the incumbent staff to take in the news.

'When did all this blow up?' Paul asked Liam Green. Liam looked as shocked as Paul felt.

'I got a call around six this morning telling me to get in at seven.'

'Me, too,' said Harry Sullivan, turning to join in the conversation.

'I had my phone switched off until I got here,' said Paul, inwardly cursing both his wife's insistence that he turn his work mobile off overnight, and his own habit of not switching it on until he got to the office in the morning.

'I wonder what they'll do?' said Liam.

'The board are likely to get their marching orders,' said Harry, 'and that puts us next in line for the chop.'

'That's all I need!' said Paul.

'You and me both,' said Liam. 'Come on, let's see who knows what before we go and face the troops. This is going to be a heck of a day.'

***

Harry's prediction turned out to be correct; within a week, the new owners had fired the entire existing board of directors and had started appointing new members, their own people. The move was, perhaps, to be expected; but that didn't make it welcome. Meanwhile his own team were pressing him for information, but he had nothing to tell them – not yet, at least. Paul knew his own fate would be decided before theirs. That was just a matter of time.

He was turning things over in his mind the following Tuesday morning when the phone rang.

He picked it up. 'Paul Wayman.'

'Hi, Paul, I'm Ed Deacon. I've been appointed to the board as the director with responsibility for your area.'

'I see. Congratulations.' Paul's heart was in his boots.

'Thank you. I'd like us to have a chat, so can you come over to my office right away? It's the one that used to belong to George Davies.'

'I'll be there in five minutes,' said Paul, fearing the worst. He stuffed his latest departmental report into his satchel, grabbed his jacket, and headed off to meet his new boss.

Paul had enjoyed a good relationship with George Davies, the director he'd reported to previously, based largely on the basis of each letting the other get on with things. He suspected that Davies' successor would be different. Certainly Harry Sullivan's new boss had already proved more demanding than the last one had been.

The door was open when Paul got to what was now Ed Deacon's office. He knocked, then went in.

Deacon was busy making notes in a leather notebook and he completed what he was doing before looking up.

'Paul, hello there.' He stood up and stuck his hand out. 'Pleased to meet you.'

'Likewise,' said Paul. Deacon was a grey-haired man dressed in a dark suit, but with no tie, he noticed.

'Sit down, won't you.' They both sat. 'Thank you for making the time to come and see me.' Ed leaned back in his chair; he looked like he was considering his next words carefully. Paul's eyes were drawn to a framed quotation on the wall behind Ed.

TAIICHI OHNO QUOTATION

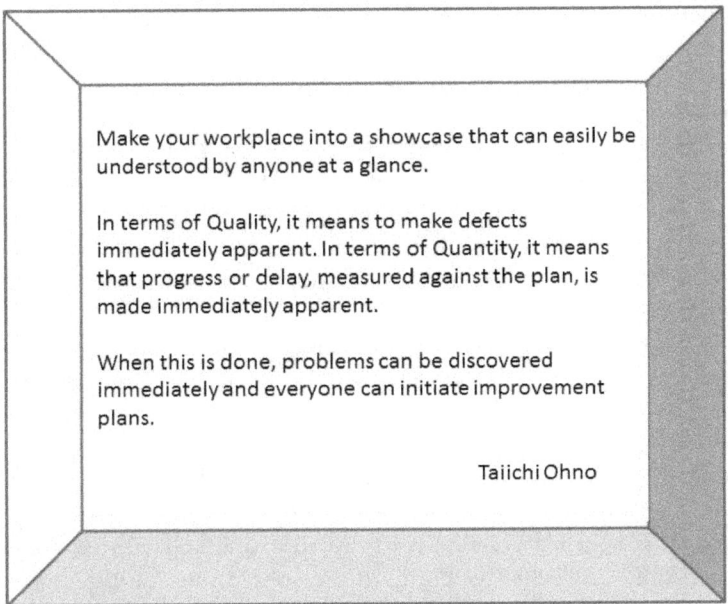

FIGURE 1

'Tell me,' Ed said at last, 'what do you think a manager in this firm must do?'

'I ... I think they must do many things,' said Paul, flustered by the question. He started reeling off a list of managerial duties. 'Set objectives, look after the team, ensure a good level of service for customers, communicate well, empower people, work hard ...'

Ed remained silent and allowed Paul to run out of ideas, then he spoke with conviction.

'You failed to mention the one thing I was looking for. A manager in this firm must deliver results. All the other things you mentioned are important, but results are of prime importance.

'I'd like to start by taking a look at the results delivered by your people. Show me what a good result looks like for you and your team, and show me the problems you need to solve to deliver these results consistently.'

Paul started to explain what his department did, intending to go on to say what they had been working on and the problems they were experiencing, but Ed quickly stopped him. 'No,' he said, shaking his head. 'I asked you to *show* me, not tell me. I want to *see* the facts.'

'I produce a report each month.'

'Show me.'

Paul reached into his satchel and pulled out a thick document. He placed it on the desk.

Ed picked up the report, flicked through it and glanced at a selection of pages. Then he shook his head and threw it back down on the desk. 'It's too long, and the charts are too complicated,' he said. 'Since it's produced monthly it'll be out of date by the time I get to read it. Besides which, if I sat here reading reports like that all day, I'd never get out of the office to see what's really going on.'

Paul put the report back in his satchel, feeling dismayed.

Ed sighed and softened his voice. 'Do you know why my company took yours over, Paul?'

Paul shook his head. 'Not really.'

'For the past two years you've not been making any money. Your profitability is poor and your cash flow's out of control. However, my people believe that this company can be made to run well, and I agree. After being here for a couple of weeks I've come to the conclusion that this business has been run strategically rather than operationally. Management has been too hands-off. What I believe is needed is hands-on, detailed, hard-driving management. We need to set targets and deadlines and be able to see that we're making rapid progress.'

Paul nodded; he wasn't entirely sure what Ed was driving at, but he wasn't going to admit it.

'Let's take a walk,' said Ed. 'Take me to where your team works and show me round.'

Paul took a deep breath and silently prayed that his team were doing everything they should be doing – and nothing that they shouldn't be.

***

After a short walk Ed and Paul arrived in the large, spacious office where Paul's team was based. Things were fairly quiet; most people had their heads down, working at computer terminals. Ed asked Paul to walk him around and point out who the people were and what they were working on.

The tour over, Ed walked to the centre of the room and looked around. 'How do I see what results this team is trying to produce?' he said. 'I can see they're all busy people, but I'd like to be able to see what their key targets are and how they are performing as a team against those targets. I'd like to see if they had a good week last week and where problems in one area are likely to affect another area in the future. I'd like to see the problems they're facing and what they are doing to resolve them.'

'They tell me if they have any problems,' said Paul. 'They're all consummate professionals, they each do a good job, and the proof of that is that I rarely have any complaints from customers.'

'If they're all doing such a great job on their own, what do we need you for?' Ed asked, then stayed silent and waited for Paul to think about what he had just said.

'I'm here to help when they have problems. I also set their objectives and appraise their progress, among other things,' replied Paul. He had a sense of impending doom.

'That's the best answer you've given me so far,' said Ed. 'Come on, let's go and get some coffee.'

Paul led the way to the coffee machine. Ed pulled some coins from his pocket and fed them into the slot, then stepped back. 'After you,' he said.

Paul selected black coffee, then Ed got himself some tea and they made their way to Paul's office. They sat at the round meeting table in the corner, rather than at his desk.

'I want to help you, Paul,' said Ed. He sipped his tea then set it down. 'I want to give you a chance, and, to do that, I'm going to set you a challenge and give you some coaching. There'll also be a timeframe in which results must be achieved.'

'Sounds good,' said Paul, feeling relieved. 'What's the challenge?'

'I want you to set up visual management for your team.'

'Visual management?' Paul had heard of it but decided not to make any assumptions. 'How do I do that?'

'That's where the coaching comes in. I want you to meet with some people at another company we took over recently. The people concerned have made great progress, they'll give you some new ideas and show you the practical steps you need to take to implement visual management. After you've seen them and learned what they have to teach you, I want you to report back to me.'

'Okay.'

Ed reached inside his jacket pocket and produced a notebook. He quickly wrote down some information, then tore out the page. 'These are the people I want you to go and see. They'll be expecting you,' he said, as he handed the page to Paul.

Paul read the information Ed had written down. There were two names – Mariam Khan and Mike Bailey – along with phone numbers.

Ed continued. 'When it comes to visual management, there are three key areas of learning. First, I need you to learn visual management techniques; second, I need you to learn the correct behaviours; and finally I need you to develop the correct leadership mindset.'

'Okay,' said Paul, folding the page and putting it in his pocket. He still wasn't sure what this was all about. Probably more management gobbledegook, just another time-intensive theory with no practical application.

Ed picked up on his reticence. 'Your first challenge will be to remain open-minded,' he said. 'I'll leave things in your hands. Call me when you have something to show me.'

Paul nodded, his expression serious.

'As for the timeframe, I'm giving you three weeks to set up effective visual management in your department. I like you, Paul; I don't want to have to replace you. Please don't disappoint me.' With that Ed left the office.

Chapter 2

Reflection and resolve

When Paul got home that evening he shut the front door behind himself with a sense of relief. After Ed had left his office, he'd put in a call to Mariam Khan and arranged to go and see her in the morning, but he had mixed feelings about the whole thing. What if he was just being set up to fail so they could justify giving him the boot? Ed didn't seem the kind who would do that, but what did he really know about him? He had no doubt the three week deadline was real enough; he'd be out of a job within the month if he didn't get to grips with this visual management thing.

The house was unnaturally quiet as he headed up to the bedroom to get changed. Rebecca, his wife, had been planning to go to her mother's house straight from work to pick up some things to take into hospital for her. The poor old lady had taken a tumble the week before and broken her hip, and, when she'd been examined, it turned out it wasn't the first time she'd fallen.

The accident couldn't have happened at a worse time; Paul and Rebecca were in the process of selling their home. Now that their two daughters were at university, they planned to move to a small village rather than living in town. It was something to which they'd been looking forward for a number of years, and the house they were buying – situated on a riverbank and with steep staircases – wasn't suitable for his mother-in-law. The hunt was now on for a good nursing home for her.

After he'd changed into casual clothes, Paul went into the kitchen and rummaged through the fridge, wondering what to cook for dinner. He decided on spaghetti bolognese; he could cook the sauce and leave the pasta until Rebecca got home.

He got out the things he needed and started by chopping onions, the simple repetitive task allowing his mind to consider the situation at work.

Paul had had many years' experience as a manager, gained in a variety of organisations. He'd worked in government offices, manufacturing, construction, and operations, sometimes for successful companies, sometimes for organisations that were struggling. He felt that management was pretty much the same everywhere; a bunch of people paid to make decisions and get results and who just did the best they could under the circumstances. How well anyone did in any particular role was pretty much a lottery – it all depended on having the right people in your team and whether your face fitted. Sometimes you won and sometimes you lost, but if you made enough decent moves and stuck it out, you would be promoted and make it to a senior level.

While continuing to cook, his mind turned to the meeting he had lined up with Mariam Khan in the morning. He wondered what form the coaching would take – whether it would be something useful, or just more theories and concepts, the management equivalent of the flavour of the month.

Paul reflected on the vast amount of personal development work he'd undertaken over the years. He had read many books and been on many training courses. They had taught him some key Japanese management phrases, and plenty of new theories. Each time he had finished a book or a course he had returned to work enthusiastic, but unsure how to implement change. The difficulty of translating concepts into practical solutions, coupled with the urgency of day-to-day duties, had diluted his enthusiasm.

I need ideas I can just go ahead and implement, he thought. *I wish someone could show me the how, not just the what, why and where: I need simple, practical solutions that can be put into practice quickly.*

Over time, Paul had become disillusioned with trying to implement new ideas for improvement in the workplace. He had settled into a quiet life of muddling through as best he could. Eventually, he became a senior manager through his age and experience, rather than his ability to deliver extraordinary results.

Paul heard the front door open and a moment later Rebecca came into the kitchen. 'What a day!' she said, as she plonked down in the seat opposite his.

Paul got to his feet and poured her a glass of wine. 'Here you go,' he said. 'Dinner's in hand, so you just relax.'

'Thanks, love,' she said. She took a sip of wine. 'I needed that!'

He put a pan of water on to boil and then joined her at the table. 'What's up?' he asked.

'Oh, it's Mum. You know she's seemed quite forgetful since she went into hospital? Well, I think that's been going on for a while now. When I was picking her things up I tidied round a bit and I found a notebook behind the cushion of her chair.' She bent down and took something out of her bag.

'Here,' she said, holding it out to him, 'take a look at that.'

Paul took the book and opened it up. There were pictures of him, Rebecca and the two girls glued down one side of the page with their names and a note of who they were written alongside. He closed the book and put it down on the table. 'Poor soul,' he said. 'Mind you, that's quite clever, don't you think?'

'I suppose so. It seems like it's been one thing after another lately, though.' She sipped her wine. 'I wonder if we're taking on more than we can chew. Do you think we should take the house off the market and stay put, at least for now?'

'No,' said Paul, 'you've set your heart on a new house, and we've been planning that for years. No. We'll manage, you'll see.'

Rebecca nodded. 'Okay, if you say so. I just feel a bit overwhelmed at the moment.'

***

After they'd eaten and Rebecca had gone for a soak in the bath, Paul's thoughts turned once more to Ed Deacon and what he meant by visual management. Paul already wrote reports full of charts and dashboard indicators of performance, but that didn't seem to be what Ed wanted. He'd shown them to him, only to have them dismissed. He remembered Ed's comment about the company having been managed strategically rather than operationally. So he started up his laptop, wanting to be sure he understood the difference clearly.

He found a useful website and read:

> Strategic management is about standing back to see the big picture of the organisation and its direction, formulating big goals and initiatives and allocating resources to implement them. Strategic objectives are broad in scope and long-term.
>
> Operational management is about the design and implementation of business practices to achieve daily, weekly and monthly objectives and targets. Operational objectives are short-term and can be used as an element of the day-to-day running of a business.
>
> While they are interlinked, if strategic objectives aren't translated into operational objectives, then goals aren't likely to be achieved.

Well, that seemed clear enough. It fitted with what Ed had said about his management having been too hands-off, and the need to set targets and deadlines so they could see that rapid progress was being made.

Throughout his career, Paul had been promoted, left to stagnate until he moved on to get a leg up, and made redundant, but right now what he needed was just to hang on to his job. With the house move, the girls at university, and his mother-in-law about to enter an expensive nursing home, he needed to maintain his income. Rebecca had enough on her plate with her mum, so he decided to keep what was happening at work to himself. If he met the challenge he'd been given, then telling her about the situation would only have worried her unnecessarily, and if he didn't there'd be time enough to worry in a few weeks.

He couldn't let it come to that, though; he had to get to grips with the situation, and in no more than three weeks.

Chapter 3

Visual management basics explained

Next morning Paul was nervous as he punched the postcode into his satnav and set off for his meeting with Mariam Khan. He soon arrived at the address and drove through a set of big old iron gates and up a long, tree-lined driveway to a large car park with just a few spaces remaining. He parked and took a moment to look at the office building. It was old and imposing, with Georgian windows and an impressive portico, and obviously well maintained. He made his way inside to the company's reception desk, where he asked for Mariam Khan. He was given a pass, directed to the stairs and told to go to the second floor where he would find her office directly to the left of the landing.

When Paul arrived at the office, he found the door standing open. A smartly dressed woman in her thirties was making notes on a whiteboard. She heard him approach, turned and smiled.

'Hello,' he said, 'are you Mariam Khan? I'm Paul Wayman. We spoke on the phone yesterday; Ed Deacon said you might be able to help me.' Paul held out his hand and Mariam took it and shook it warmly.

'Yes, I can help you,' she said. 'Let's take a walk. I need to start by showing you something.'

Around the corner from Mariam Khan's office was a large open plan area. They walked through it to a room without a door, an annex to the main office. The room was square and white walled. At the far end was a colourful display of charts and graphs, all computer generated (refer to Figure 2 for the overview; detail is shown in Figures 2a to 2g).

VISUAL DISPLAY

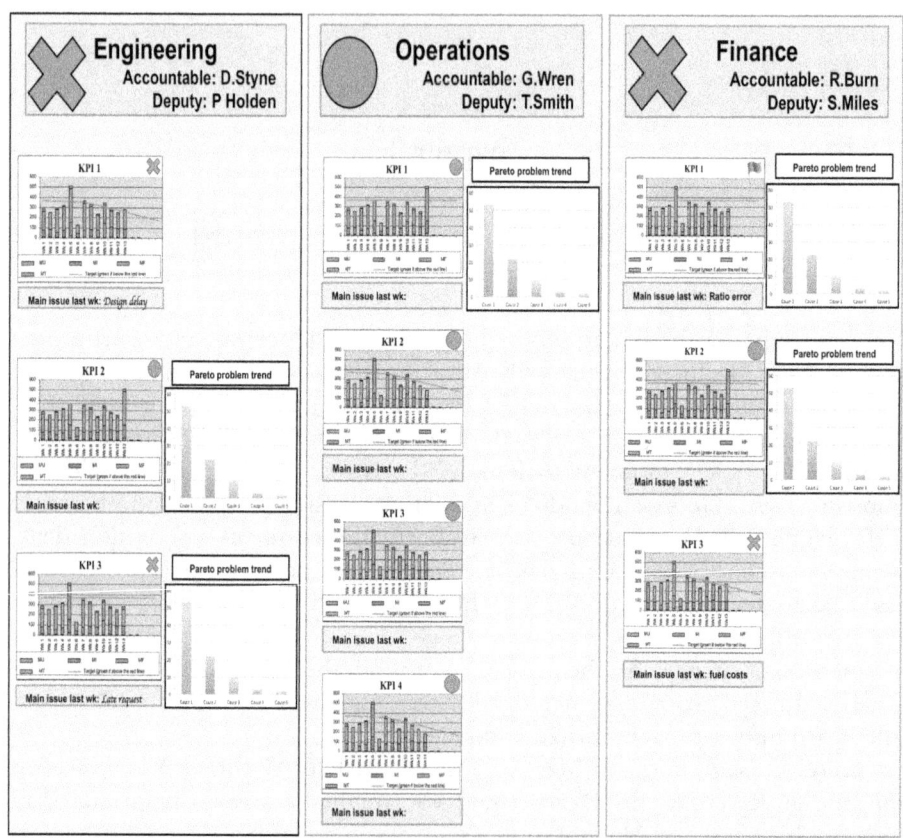

FIGURE 2

VISUAL DISPLAY – KPI CHART STATUS

 RED – Below target / standard

 GREEN – Meets or exceeds target / standard

 RED FLAG – Risk needing proactive action

FIGURE 2a

VISUAL DISPLAY – FINANCE DETAIL

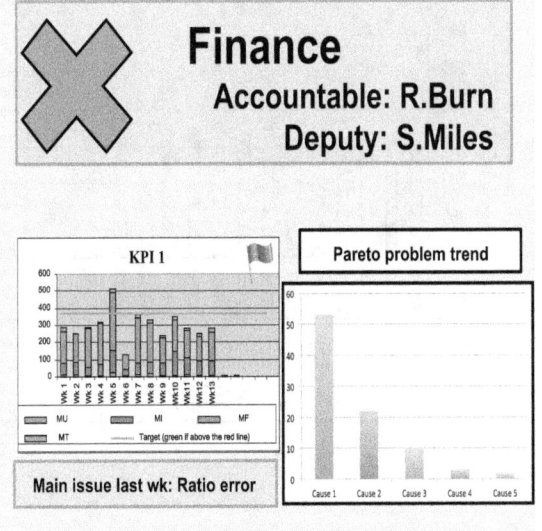

FIGURE 2b

VISUAL DISPLAY – OPERATIONS DETAIL

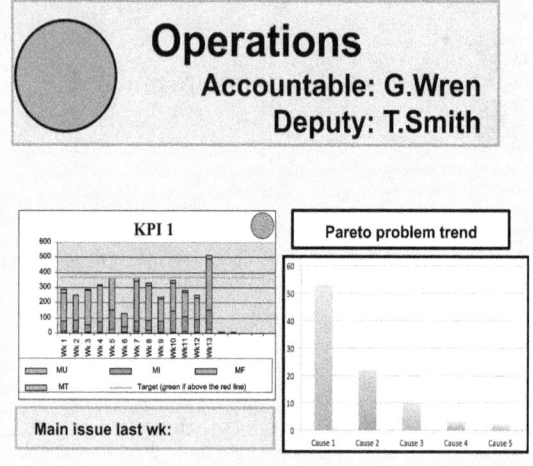

FIGURE 2c

VISUAL DISPLAY – OPERATIONS KPI 1 DETAIL

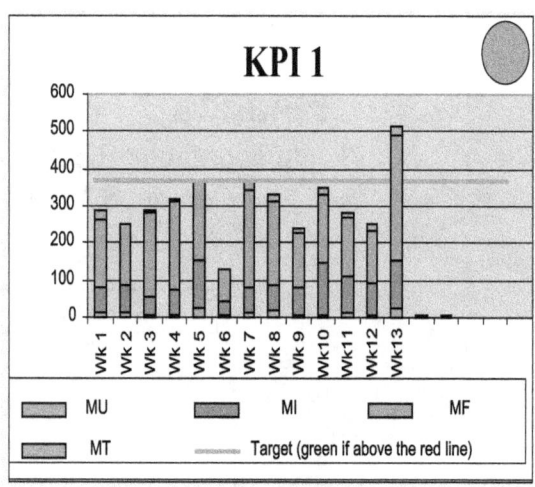

FIGURE 2d

VISUAL DISPLAY – FINANCE KPI 3 DETAIL

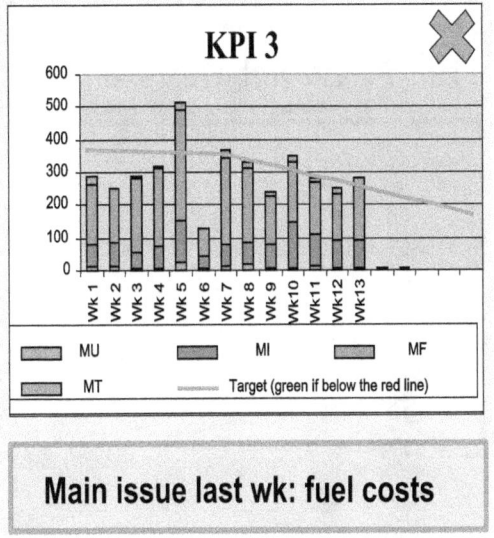

FIGURE 2e

VISUAL DISPLAY – ENGINEERING KPI 1 DETAIL

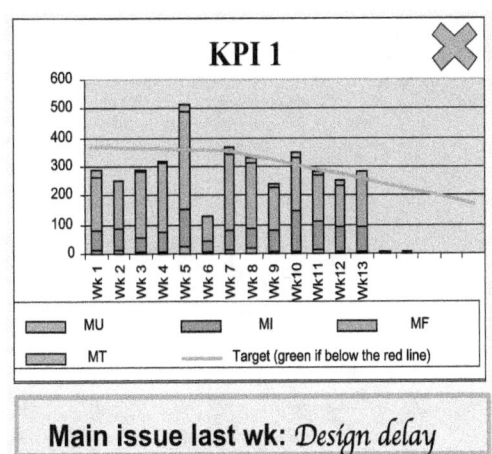

FIGURE 2f

VISUAL DISPLAY – PARETO PROBLEM TREND DETAIL

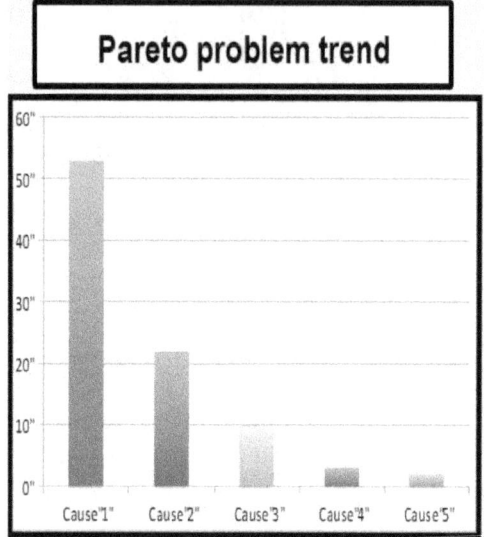

FIGURE 2g

There was also a second visual display on the left hand wall; it contained the same information, but was filled in by hand rather than computer generated (refer to Figures 3, 3a, 3b).

THE VISUAL MANAGER

VISUAL DISPLAY – HIGH TOUCH, LOW TECH

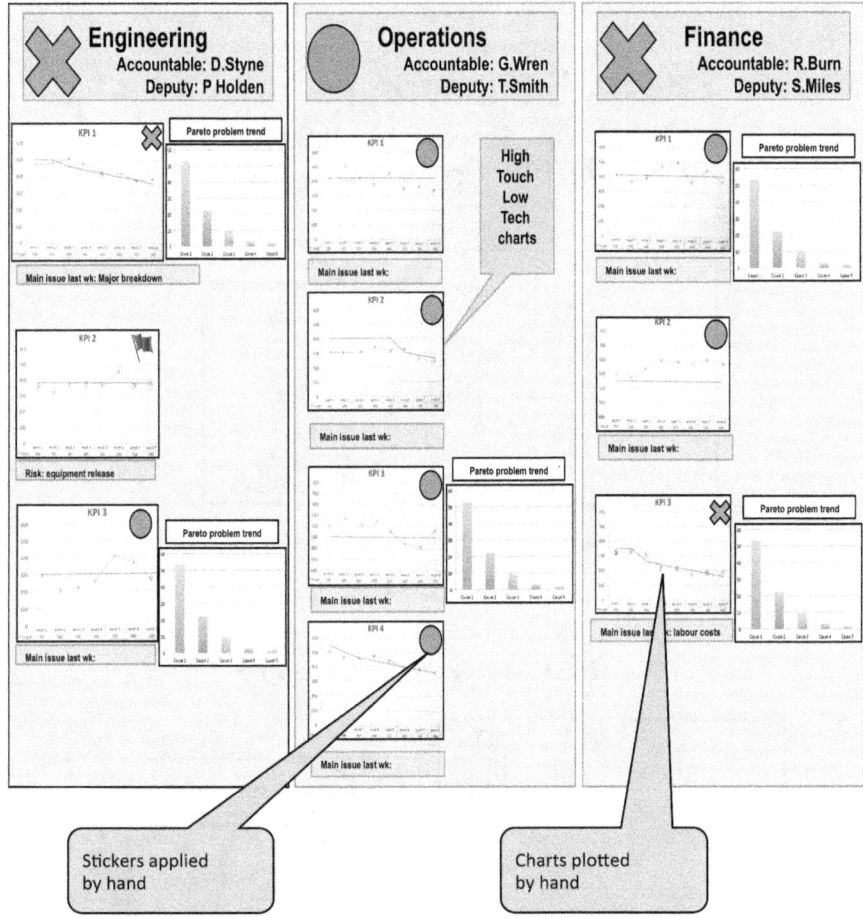

FIGURE 3

VISUAL DISPLAY – HIGH TOUCH, LOW TECH, ENGINEERING DETAIL – KPI 1

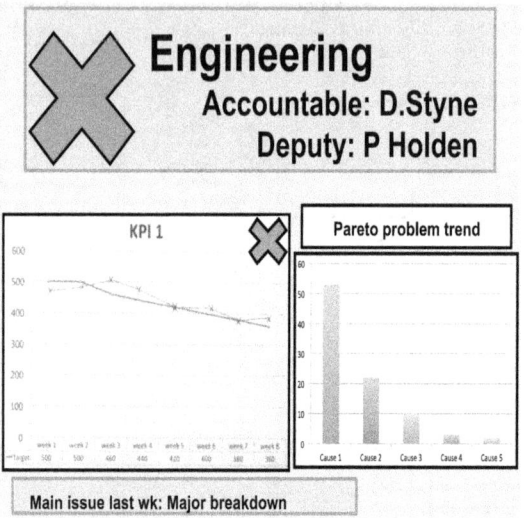

FIGURE 3a

VISUAL DISPLAY – HIGH TOUCH, LOW TECH, ENGINEERING DETAIL– KPI 3

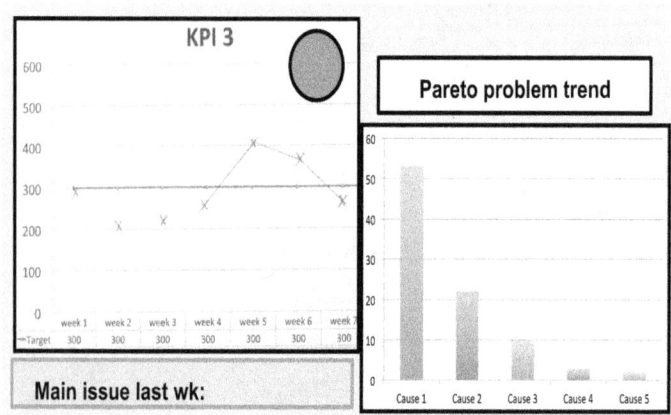

FIGURE 3b

On the right hand wall was a large whiteboard, again filled in by hand, and with a large heading: 'Actions' (refer to Figures 4, 4a and 5).

ACTIONS BOARD

ID #	Date	Area	Problem	Containment / Countermeasure	Owner	Date	Status
1	1.3	Ops	Productivity KPI below target caused by B3x2 project on hold due to layout drawings out of date	Containment - urgent update of drawings and overtime to catch back time lost. Countermeasure - 5 why = no scheduled design review of infrastructure layout changes - implement scheduled design review	GW	8.1	●
ID #	Date	Area #	Problem	Containment / Countermeasure	Owner	Date	Status
2	1.3	Ops	Delivery performance KPI below target caused by Plans rejected by safety committee	Containment - arrange urgent stakeholder meeting Countermeasure - 5 why = decision making criteria not understood - investigate and build into standard for constructing future plans	GW	8.1	●
ID #	Date	Area #	Problem	Containment / Countermeasure	Owner	Date	Status
3	3.4	Eng	Maintenance KPI below target caused by lack of personnel - too many people on holiday at the same time.	Containment - Over time to catch back Countermeasure - 5 why = No standard for holiday booking - create standard, sign off and introduce	DS	10.4	◐
ID #	Date	Area #	Problem	Containment / Countermeasure	Owner	Date	Status
4	3.4	Eng	Engineering tool refurb KPI below target caused by Design Delay	Containment - urgent design release to allow catchback	DS	10.4	◔
ID #	Date	Area #	Problem	Containment / Countermeasure	Owner	Date	Status
5	3.4	Fin	Assets KPI predicted to be below target for 2nd quarter caused by ratio error	Containment - investigate and correct Countermeasure - 5 why = Lack of standardised procedure for ratio calculation for all accountants - create standard	SM	10.4	◕
ID #	Date	Area #	Problem	Containment / Countermeasure	Owner	Date	Status
6	3.4	Fin	Cost KPI below target caused by greater than expected fuel costs	Containment - All managers to monitor fuel usage and reduce by consolidating transport. Countermeasure - investigate and create a breakdown of reasons for high fuel cost - create pareto + 5 why	SM	10.4	◔

Problem Understood	Containment / Countermeasure Action Agreed	Agree Action In Progress	Action Complete
◔	◐	◕	●

FIGURE 4

Actions Board – Close Detail

ID #	Date	Area #	Problem
6	3.4	Fin	Cost KPI below target caused by greater than expected fuel costs

Containment / Countermeasure	Owner	Date	Status
Containment - All managers to monitor fuel usage and reduce by consolidating transport. Countermeasure - Investigate and create a breakdown of reasons for high fuel cost - create pareto + 5 why	SM	10.4	

FIGURE 4a

ACTIONS – PRO FORMA EXAMPLE

ID#	Date	Area#	Problem	Containment/Countermeasure	Owner	Date	Status
							⊕
ID#	Date	Area#	Problem	Containment/Countermeasure	Owner	Date	Status
							⊕
ID#	Date	Area#	Problem	Containment/Countermeasure	Owner	Date	Status
							⊕

Problem Understood   Containment/Countermeasure Agreed   Agreed Action In Progress   Action Complete

FIGURE 5

Paul focused on the display on the back wall (refer to Figure 2) and saw that it was divided into three sections headed 'Engineering', 'Operations' and 'Finance'. Beneath each department heading was the name of an accountable person and their deputy.

'This is my top level visualisation room,' said Mariam. 'The display you can see on the back wall is a snapshot of my directorate's performance. As a director I have very little time and need to be able to see quickly how well my three departments are performing. Ed calls this "status at a glance". At a glance I can understand a great deal of information about my team's performance. All managers and directors in this business use a principle called One, Three, Ten.'

'What's that?'

'It's simple I want to be able to see where the problem areas are in one second. In three seconds I want to know what the problems are, and in ten I want to understand what actions are currently being taken to address those problems.'

Paul stood back and took a good hard look at the display. 'Can you give me an example of what this tells you?' he asked.

'Of course,' said Mariam Khan. 'The display can look strange and confusing when you're not used to it, but when I stand back ten feet, the first thing I look at is the very top. Do you see the red crosses and green circles next to each department's name?'

'Yes, I can see those.'

'The red "X" next to the title "Engineering" means that the engineering department missed one or more of their targets over the last week, whereas the green "O" next to the title "Operations" means that the operations department hit all theirs.'

'I see,' said Paul; he looked at the third section. 'So the finance department also missed one or more of its targets, because it also has a red "X" at the top next to their title.'

'That's exactly right.'

'Is that all it tells you, or can you see more?'

'I can see a lot more,' said Mariam. 'For example, if I see a red "X" next to the department name, I then look at the KPI charts below.' (Refer to Appendix 1.) 'Do you see where?' (Refer to Figures 2b-2g.) Paul nodded. 'Each KPI chart represents the tracking of a particular Key Performance Indicator and also has a red "X" or a green "O" in the top corner. The visual display contains all the vital KPIs for each department.

'Each KPI on our visual display has a specific target level to be achieved. If the chart shows a red "X" in the top corner then that KPI is below target.' She glanced at Paul to be sure he was following, then continued. 'If we look at engineering, for example, we can see that they have three KPIs. Two of them have Red "X"s and one of them has a green "O". This means that engineering has missed two targets and hit one over the last week.'

Paul nodded and then frowned, a little puzzled.

'I don't understand why you need the red "X"s and green "O"s. Surely you can work out if the KPIs are on or off target by studying the charts?'

'I could,' she said, 'but that would take a lot longer and would no longer give me status at a glance. I want to use as much of my time as possible coaching people and supporting them to solve problems, rather than trying to work out what is going on and where the problems lie. You'll understand the power of this idea when you attend a review meeting.' (Refer to Appendix 6.)

'Oh, okay.'

'There's one more symbol I need to show you,' said Mariam. 'Can you see that, on the top chart of the finance sections, there's a red flag?' (Refer to Figure 2b.)

'Yes, I can see that. Is that the same as a red X?'

'No. The red flag indicates a risk, a problem looming in the future. A red flag shows you need to act now to stop the risk from growing.'

'Right, so it's something you can prevent from becoming a red "X".'

'That's right. As you can see there are two visual displays in this room (Refer to Figures 2 & 3). One of them is our old one and shows how we got started with visual management. The other one is our current working display and is a significant improvement on the old one. Can you tell me which is the old display and which is the new one, and why you think that?'

Paul considered the two and made up his mind quickly. He pointed to the one on the left hand wall (Figure 3). 'I reckon that one is the old one,' he said, 'because the charts have been updated by hand using coloured pens. The new one (Figure 2) has all the charts updated on a computer and printed out. It looks neater and more professional. I'm sure the old one was functional, but it doesn't look half as smart.'

Mariam looked at Paul and laughed. 'I thought that's what you might say,' she said, 'because that's what most people say. Actually, the smart looking one is our old one and the display updated by hand is our current working version.' (Refer to Figures 3 & 6.)

VISUAL DISPLAY – HIGH TOUCH, LOW TECH
(MAINTENANCE SCHEDULE)

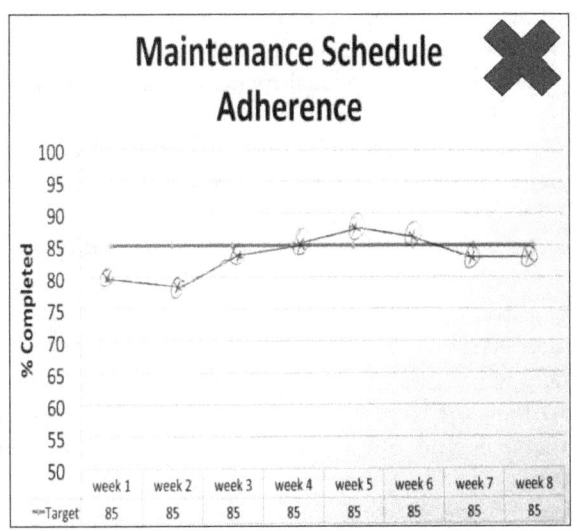

FIGURE 6

'It may not look as pretty but it is equally functional. We call the latest version "low tech, high touch".

'The reason we switched to it was because updating by hand is so much quicker. The problem with the computer printout version was that it took a long time to update each week. My managers complained they didn't have the time to do it – they wanted me to hire an admin guy to fix that. I didn't want to bear the cost and anyway I wanted to keep responsibility with my managers. With the new system they come here every Monday morning and update the visual display using nothing more than coloured pens, and it only takes fifteen minutes to do. There's no need to remove the charts from the wall, reprint them and pin them back up.'

'Great idea.'

'I think so. Some of the managers initially complained about needing extra time to collect the data, but I pushed back because I expect them to know the status of their departments each week. I expect them to have hands-on knowledge of where they are in relation to their targets, what the problems are and what they're doing to sort them out.'

'Sounds right. It's stuff they need to be on top of, to do their job.'

'Exactly. And the proof that they value this is that they've set up their own visual management with each of their supervisors. Many of the supervisors now run daily visual management to make sure they have a tight level of control over their day-to-day operations.'

Paul was surprised, but he had to admit it made sense. He'd been starting to worry about how much time visual management was going to require, but Mariam had shown him a way that was very efficient.

Mariam paused and then said, 'You've just learned an important rule of visual management, Paul. You've got to use status at a glance and pass the One, Three, Ten test.'

'By putting a red "X" or a green "O" in the top corner of each individual chart to show at a glance whether it is on target or off target for the current period?', Paul replied.

Mariam nodded. 'And in addition, the whole visual display must also show status at a glance, which we achieve by putting a red "X" or a green "O" at the top, next to the department's name. A green "O" is placed next to the department's name if, and only if, all KPI charts for the department have green "O" status.'

'Can you talk me through one of the KPI charts?'

'Sure,' said Mariam. 'Would you like to pick one? Then I'll explain it to you.'

Paul looked over the charts and pointed to one in the engineering section. 'How about that one; what does that tell you?'

'That chart represents the KPI for the engineers' adherence to the maintenance schedule,' said Mariam. (Refer to Figure 6.) 'The engineers are scheduled to check and maintain a set number of assets each week. This is important because well-maintained assets enable the operations department to reliably deliver services to our customers. You can see the target line is a straight line, because we have a set target to achieve each week. Unfortunately, the current chart has a red "X" in the corner and that means the engineers have missed their weekly target.'

'Who set the target?' asked Paul, wondering if it was simply a case of the target being unrealistic.

'The engineers did,' said Mariam, setting that theory to rest. 'The target was set by them and then agreed with me.'

'Does that mean the engineers get into trouble?' asked Paul, starting to feel a little uncomfortable.

'No,' said Mariam. She smiled. 'A red "X" means that we have an opportunity to improve by identifying the issue that is stopping us from hitting our target. If you look closely, you will see that the engineers have written notes below the chart to describe the main problems they have. I'll expect them to identify the actions they need to take to get back on target and also whether any action is required to prevent a recurrence of the problem. Actions are written on the board on the right hand wall.' (Refer to Figure 4.)

'I see.'

'We are tough on problems and the causes of problems, Paul, but we are supportive of people. We believe that problems are caused by bad processes, not by bad people. The red "X" is showing up a process problem, not a people problem. Mind you, that doesn't mean that we are a soft touch. As directors and managers, we challenge our people to solve process problems and we also coach and support them to help them to do that. We're tough but fair. This is how we drive continuous improvement.'

'That seems reasonable,' said Paul. He continued to study the visual display and then said, 'There are other charts to the right of some of the KPI charts, and they don't have red "X"s or green "O"s. Can you tell me what those are for?'

'Those are Pareto charts; we use them where selected KPIs need focused improvement.' (Refer to Figure 7.)

PARETO CHART

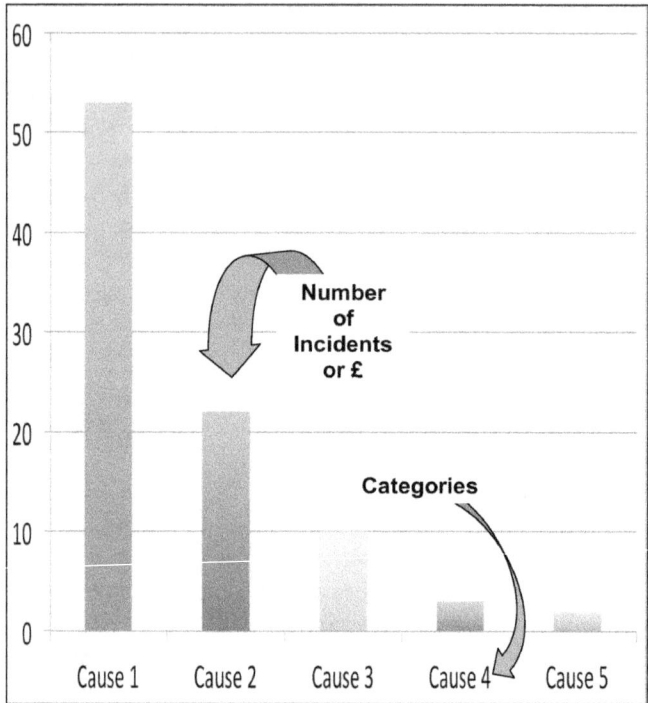

FIGURE 7

'You're familiar with the eighty-twenty rule?' (Refer to Appendix 2.) Paul nodded. 'Well, the Pareto charts show the main problems we need to solve to improve selected KPIs, the vital few rather than the trivial many, as Joseph Juran might have put it.

'I've already explained how I expect my team to take action to address red KPIs and get back on track. Unfortunately, quick actions are sometimes not enough to improve a red KPI. For that, my team collects data and builds up a record of all problems, both big and small. Over time these records start to produce a picture of the top five most damaging problems that are repeating.'

'How do you know for sure what they are?'

'The basic underlying rule behind the Pareto chart is that only a small number of repeating problems will account for a large majority of KPI failures. This is useful because we can see where we need to focus our efforts. We only need to solve a small number of problems to get a big improvement in our KPI.'

'Can you give me an example?'

'Of course,' said Mariam. She walked over to the flip chart and flipped over the pages until she found a blank sheet. She picked up a pen and turned to face Paul.

'Let's say that my department processes application forms from customers. We set ourselves a target to successfully process at least ninety per cent of the application forms each week. We set up our visual display with a KPI chart and we start to track the percentage of application forms successfully processed each week. After only two weeks we start to miss the target, although at this stage we don't know whether the problem is acute or chronic.'

'What's the difference?' (Refer to Appendix 3.)

'As you know from experience, day-to-day or week-to-week problems affecting targets come and go; they are the acute problems and are due to something specific that has had a bad effect on performance. An example of an acute problem might be that a member of staff is ill or the delivery of application forms is delayed because of a traffic problem. Chronic problems are problems built into the process. They're often insidious and may even be covered up by the acute problem of the day or week, which is why data needs to be collected over a longer period of time to show their full effect.

'Acute problems tend to be one off problems that need quick actions to contain and fix them. If they are serious enough and there is a risk of a repeat, they may also need root cause analysis and solution, but they are visible and the first step is quick action.

'Chronic problems tend to be concealed and repeating. They need data to be collected over a longer period of time, which makes them visible on a Pareto chart, and then they need to be addressed using root cause analysis.' (Refer to Appendix 4.)

'Going back to our example, say we agree actions to address all the acute problems, but we still keep missing the target. That suggests a chronic issue and so we agree there's a need to collect data and create a Pareto chart to understand what is driving our KPI problem.'

Paul nodded.

'We start to collect the reasons for the target being missed. We do this by asking the staff who process the forms to record the problems they experience while doing their job. After a short while we start to see a few problems repeating, so we set up a simple tick chart which looks like this.'

Mariam drew a diagram on the flip chart.

'Each person in the team has their own tick chart. Every time they have a problem with an application and it is due to something listed on the chart, they put a tick against it. If they have a problem that is not listed on the chart, then they tick "other". It takes very little time to do and doesn't affect their capacity to do their job. At the end of the week, the tick charts are collected together and all the information is compiled into one chart. That chart looks like this.' Mariam added to the information she'd sketched on the flip chart (refer to Figure 8).

MARIAM KHAN'S PARETO EXAMPLE

Team member A		Total
Can't Read	✓✓	2
No Address	✓✓	2
Missing Info	✓	1
Not Signed	✓✓	2
Other	✓	1

Team member B		Total
Can't Read	✓✓✓	3
No Address	✓✓✓	3
Missing Info	✓	1
Not Signed	✓✓✓✓✓✓	6
Other	✓	1

Team member C		Total
Can't Read	✓✓	2
No Address	✓✓✓✓	4
Missing Info	✓	1
Not Signed	✓✓✓✓✓✓✓✓✓	9
Other		0

Pareto Chart — Application Form Problems (bar chart showing Number of ticks for: Not Signed, No Address, Can't Read, Missing Info, Other)

FIGURE 8

'As you can see, a pattern is developing and the chart is starting to look like a Pareto chart.'

'Yes, I see,' said Paul.

'Two weeks later the chart looks like this,' she said, adding more information, 'and as you can see the positions of the problems are staying the same.' (Refer to Figure 8a.)

MARIAM KHAN'S PARETO EXAMPLE (TWO WEEKS LATER)

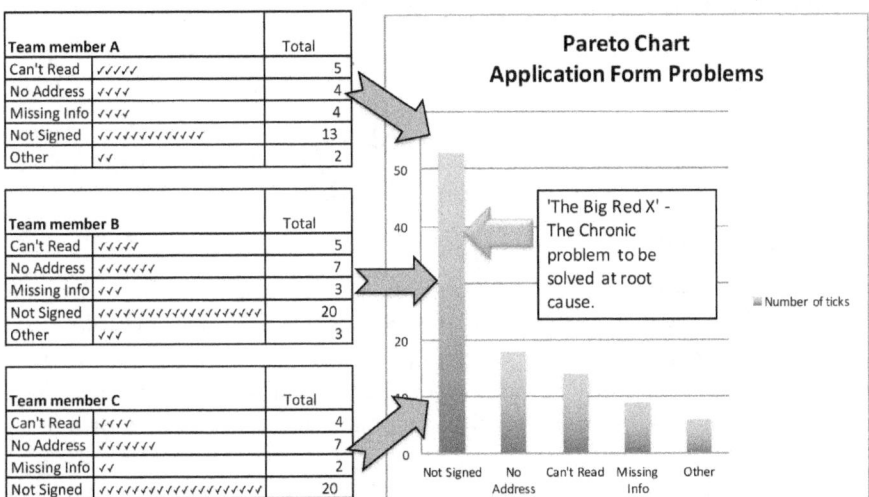

FIGURE 8a

'We now know the vital few chronic problems to be solved and at this stage I would start to coach the team in problem-solving methods to help them identify the root cause of the problem having the biggest impact on the KPI. That's the primary cause, which Dorian Shainin described as "the Big Red X". Once we solve the first problem on the Pareto chart and apply a countermeasure, then the KPI chart immediately starts to improve.

'You may have noticed, Paul, that the action board shows both containment and countermeasure actions. A countermeasure is an action that addresses the root cause of a problem. This is different from a containment action, which is usually a rapid action to address the symptoms. Both containment and countermeasure actions are important for different reasons. Containment actions are usually quick to identify and can be put in place quickly. Countermeasures are slower to identify and implement, but address the root cause to stop problems from reoccurring.'

Mariam's phone buzzed and she glanced at the display. 'I need to take this call. I'd also like to give you some time to make some notes, as I've given you lot of information. I believe the best test of understanding is the ability to summarise clearly and simply. When I come back, I'll review your notes with you.'

She left the room and Paul pulled his notebook from his pocket and began to write.

***

Paul's notebook entry
VISUAL MANAGEMENT

The Visual Display

Status at a glance – By standing back from the visual display I can understand the status of my team in ten seconds. In one second I want to be able to see where the problem areas are; in three seconds I want to be able to understand what the problems are; and in ten seconds I want to be able to understand what actions are currently being taken to address those problems.

Advantages – Saves time understanding where the team are on target and where they are off target and having problems. Quick grasp of the main problems that are preventing the team from hitting their targets. Provides more time to coach the team.

a) A red 'X' at the top of the visual display means that one or more of the KPIs below have missed their target for the current period of review (weekly or daily). A green 'O' at the top of the visual display means that all KPIs are on target for the current period.
b) Each KPI chart will show a red 'X' or a green 'O' in its top corner, depending on whether it is off target or on target for the current period.
c) A red flag indicated a risk. Proactive action is required.
d) High touch, low tech – by using simple, printed pro-forma charts we can quickly fill in the KPI charts by hand. This reduces time needed to update the visual display each week.
e) For selected KPI charts we use a Pareto chart to show the top three to five biggest problems we need to solve to improve performance. This chart represents the trend of problems since the start of the year.

Problem-solving is focused on the Pareto chart problems, because solving them will have the biggest impact on target achievement. We select the biggest problem – the biggest bar on the Pareto chart – to solve first.

***

Mariam Khan returned just as Paul finished taking photographs of the visual displays. 'How are you getting on?' she asked.

'Okay, I think. Here, see for yourself.' Paul passed her his notebook.

She took it and read what he had written, then looked up.

'That's an excellent summary,' she said. 'I'll let Ed know that you've made a good start in visual management.'

'I think I probably have enough ideas to get started with my team,' said Paul.

'You've learned some practical techniques and you do have enough to get started,' said Mariam, nodding. 'However, you'll also need to understand the behaviours and the leadership mindset before you're ready to make a real success of visual management.'

'Can I ask you a question about Ed?'

'Of course.'

'Is he really as tough as he seems?'

'Yes, he is. Ed believes that many people simply don't have the skills or talent for effective management. He won't waste time with people that can't quickly show they have what it takes. You've got to show him you can both deliver results and deliver them in the right way, and the right way to deliver results is to develop your team's processes, because Ed believes that the right process gives the right result. Visual management will help you achieve this.'

'What happens to the people that don't have the right skills and talent?' asked Paul.

'Ed says goodbye to them,' said Mariam.

Paul swallowed; he knew she wasn't joking.

'Thanks for your time this morning,' he said, as they shook hands. The two parted company and Paul headed off.

During his journey back to his office, Paul reflected on what he had just learned from Mariam Khan. Visual management seemed to be a fairly straightforward and practical method. *All I need to do*, he thought, *is to get my team to stick the information they already have on their computers on the wall and add some symbols.* He couldn't see the point in going to visit Mike Bailey because he felt he already understood what he needed to do. He resolved to pull his team together the next day and make a start. He would show Ed that he didn't need three weeks, he would have visual management up and running within one week.

JON MORETON

Chapter 4

First steps in visual management

'Okay everyone, I know you're all worried about this recent takeover.' Paul walked around the meeting room making eye contact with each of his team in turn. 'I wish I could tell you that everything is fine and it's just business as usual with a new logo. Unfortunately, however, our new owners are a lot more demanding and hands-on than our old ones.'

There were eight people in the room besides Paul – his four heads of department and their four deputies. As he paused to consider his next statement he noticed how quiet they had become. Everyone remained very still, their faces apprehensive.

'We've been set a challenge by our new director, Ed Deacon. He wants us to set up something called visual management. Yesterday, I visited one of our new sister companies to get to grips with what visual management is all about. I now know what's expected of us and I've taken some photographs to show to you.'

Paul switched off the lights and clicked a button on his laptop. An overhead projector beamed a photograph of Mariam Khan's display onto the white wall at the back of the room.

'This is called a visual display. It gives a snapshot of all the most important KPIs for each department and the weekly performance against each of them.'

Paul continued to explain the concept of status at a glance and the one, three, ten principle. He summarised how actions needed to be taken against missed targets and how Pareto charts were used to visualise the vital few persistent and recurring problems.

When he had finished, Paul switched on the lights. 'This is what is expected of us. We need to get on to it right away.' He walked around the room, resisting the temptation to break the silence, letting people think things through.

Sarah Parker, the operations manager, was the first to speak. 'We already produce reports,' she said. 'Why don't we just send Ed a copy of the reports we produce? And in any case, all the information he wants is visible on my PC; he can come and have a look anytime he wants to.'

Here it comes, thought Paul, bracing himself for his team's resistance to this new idea.

'I've already explained that to Ed,' said Paul, 'and I showed him our monthly report. He doesn't like it. It's too complicated, too long, and produced monthly, not weekly. Also, our reports aren't visible in the workplace and they don't use status at a glance. He doesn't count information on your PC because it is not visible and available for everyone to see.'

'We have better things to do than to stick pictures on the wall,' said Helen Jones, the engineering manager. 'I, for one, don't have time to mess about with a flavour of the month idea like this.'

'We need to find time,' said Paul, interrupting the grumbling that had broken out. 'Ed is telling, he's not asking. I don't like it any more than you do, but he's the boss. We've already seen how ruthless these people can be.'

The tension in the room was palpable; Paul suspected it wouldn't be long before everyone started to think of reasons why they couldn't or shouldn't do what he'd asked. The negativity was spreading and he needed to move the meeting forward.

'Starting from today,' he said, 'We'll write no more reports. That'll give us quite a lot of extra time, which we can use for visual management. Also, Mariam Khan showed me a technique called high touch, low tech, whereby we fill in the visual management data by hand. This will minimise the time we spend updating charts.'

Simon Brown, health and safety deputy, put his hand up. 'Yes, Simon,' said Paul.

'This will mean I have to know the KPI status of the department every week,' he said. 'That will mean a lot of extra work and time.'

Momentarily thrown off track, Paul soon recovered and said, 'Isn't that your job, Simon, to know what is going on in your own department?'

Simon realised the implications of what he had just said and put his head down. 'Well, yes, I suppose so,' he mumbled.

'As Sarah already pointed out,' said Paul, 'you already have all the information you need on your computers. All you have to do is to stick it on the wall and add the symbols to show status at a glance. Starting from 2 p.m. today, I'll be holding a series of one-to-one meetings with each head of department. Before that meeting I expect each of you, with the input of your deputy, to identify the three most important KPIs for your department.'

Paul picked up a piece of paper from the desk and handed it to Helen, who was nearest. 'This is the schedule. Please come to my office at your appointed time. Bring along your KPIs; these will then be visualised for your department.' He paused while the team passed around the schedule and each scribbled down their time slot. Then he gave them some good news. 'As you know, we have two undergraduates on work placement, Stuart and Graham; to help get the project off the ground, I've enlisted their help with setting up the visual display. Are there any more questions?'

There were a few sighs and shakes of the head, but everyone remained silent.

'See you all later then. This meeting is finished.' Paul switched off the overhead projector, disconnected his laptop, picked it up and walked out of the room.

***

During the course of the afternoon Paul's department heads turned up at their appointed times and presented their selection of KPIs to be visualised. He accepted their submissions gratefully and passed the information on to the students for construction of the displays.

Paul allocated a large area of wall space in the office for the displays, and the following morning Stuart and Graham went to work. First they divided the wall space into four sections using strips of tape. Each section was headed with a departmental title: Safety, Operations, Engineering, and Customer Service. The names of the department heads and their deputies were pinned up directly below those headings.

Next, they took the information they'd been given and began to create charts for the KPIs. As each was printed out it was stuck in place on the wall. Before the end of the day, each department had a fully populated display.

After a relentless series of meetings, Paul finally found the time mid-afternoon to go and see how things were coming along. He was pleasantly surprised that the construction was completed. Even though the charts lacked uniformity, they were a step forward.

Paul returned to his office and wrote an email to Stuart and Graham, thanking them for their efforts and asking them to print and laminate a number of red 'X's, green 'O's and red flags, and to put them in the visual display area, ready to be placed on the charts.

He next sent a brief email to his team members, informing them that the visual display was in place and requesting that they each update it with the latest status of their departments.

Finally, before he headed home for the weekend, he sent an email to Ed Deacon, letting him know that he had set up visual management in his department and inviting him to come and have a look.

***

The following Monday Paul was in his office, trawling through emails, most of which were copies of information sent to other people, when there was a knock at the door and Ed walked straight in.

'Good morning, Paul. Got your email! Looks like you've made quick progress with your team's visual management.'

'We've made a start,' said Paul. 'It was information we already had on computers, we just needed to make it visual.'

'Let's go and have a look, then.'

They walked together to the office and Paul directed Ed over to the wall where the visual display had been set up. Paul was thankful that his team had worked to his instructions; they had each updated their charts and pinned on the symbols.

Ed stood back from the visual display. 'Let's see what status at a glance tells us,' he said, as he looked over the information. 'Well, well, well, each of your departments is green, I see. There's not a red "X" or a red flag to be seen. You obviously don't have any problems. Amazing!'

Paul started to feel a sense of relief and a little smugness also crept in.

Ed moved closer to the visual display and bent forward to study the operations charts.

'The people in your team are very intelligent,' he said. 'This chart is so complicated, even Einstein would find it a challenge to understand. Who set the targets for the KPIs?'

'My heads of department set their own KPI targets,' Paul replied.

'Mmm, I thought so.' Ed reached inside his jacket pocket and drew out a piece of paper. He carefully unfolded it and handed it to Paul. 'I think you need to read this,' he said. 'A customer emailed us this. He's claiming against a penalty clause, due to late delivery of our products. Late delivery by your department, I might add.' Ed paused. 'The penalty costs will wipe out all of our profits for this month.'

Paul swallowed; he kept his eyes on the email, not reading it, just avoiding eye contact with Ed.

Ed pointed at the visual display. 'If all your departments are green and on target, how did this happen?'

Paul had no idea what to say. He felt both embarrassed by and angry with his team.

'The display you have here is very nice wallpaper, but it doesn't tell the truth, does it? What it's telling me right now is that you don't have a hands-on grasp of your own operations.' Ed sighed. 'I appreciate the attempt, Paul, and I can see you've grasped the concepts of status at a glance and high touch, low tech. But, as I explained at our first meeting, visual management is composed of three key elements: techniques, behaviours and mindset. You've started to demonstrate techniques, but you're a long way from demonstrating the other two. I want you to talk to your team and then come to my office at 4 p.m. today.'

With that, Ed walked away.

***

Paul's team shuffled into the boardroom, the only place available for their meeting. Paul sat at the centre of one of the longer sides of the boardroom table and watched silently as his department heads made their way into the room, conscious that the glass walls made them visible to onlookers.

Once everybody was seated, Paul stood up. He took the sheet of paper Ed had given him, opened it up and read out the complaint from the customer. He placed it on the table, remaining silent and glaring at the four people seated at the other side of the table.

'Would somebody like to explain to me why every KPI on our visual display is green and yet we have just let a customer down and been charged the equivalent of a month's profit as a result?' he asked.

Sarah was the first to respond. 'I'm sorry, Paul, but due to the takeover I've been focusing most on achieving high efficiencies. I maximised my efficiencies this week by focusing on the biggest customer order with the highest value. I left my smaller orders to the last minute and that customer's order,' she pointed to the paper on the table, 'was one of the smaller ones. I didn't realise it had a big penalty clause attached to it. We were only late because I was let down by engineering: they were servicing my equipment and I needed it back.'

'Why didn't your delivery performance KPI have a red X on it?' asked Paul. 'Or at least a red flag to show it was a risk.'

Sarah shrugged, 'I set my target at ninety per cent,' she said. 'I achieved ninety-two per cent. I want to show success, not failure.'

Paul groaned and turned his attention to Brian West.

'Brian, you are the head of customer service. Why didn't you see there was a problem looming? Don't you get worried when a customer order is left until the last possible minute?'

Brian started to mumble.

'Speak up,' said Paul, 'I can't hear a word you are saying.'

Brian pulled his thoughts together. 'I don't measure customer orders, Paul,' he said, 'I only measure customer feedback. I'll have a red X next week because of that email.'

'That's too late,' said Paul in exasperation. 'The horse has already bolted.'

Paul turned to Helen Jones, head of engineering. 'Helen, how come you let operations down by servicing their equipment late? Surely you could see it would cause them a problem?'

'That's not fair,' said Helen. 'We'd been waiting for that piece of equipment to be released by operations for over two months. We have a legal obligation to make sure it's serviced for safety reasons. Because it hadn't been serviced for such a long time, it took longer than expected. If it was so important, why did Operations take the risk? Why didn't they wait until they had finished that customer order before they let us have the equipment?'

An argument broke out between Sarah and Helen. Paul didn't understand most of what they were shouting at each other, but he did pick up on Helen's statement when she shouted at Sarah, 'I told you this might happen again.' Paul let it go; he wanted to focus on the way forward, not dwell on the past.

'Stop this now,' he said. He looked at each of his people in turn. 'This is a disaster, and you're responsible for it.'

Sarah, Helen and Brian all sat looking depressed. Only Peter Young, the health and safety manager, looked unaffected by the discussion.

Paul turned to him. 'Peter,' he said, 'as the head of safety, don't you monitor equipment safety and flag up when equipment is getting close to legal service requirements?'

'No,' said Peter, 'I only record accidents and information about near misses.'

Paul shook his head in disbelief. He was lost for words and could feel a headache stating to develop.

'Okay,' he said, 'let's leave it there for now. Please check that this problem doesn't happen again, and if there are any more nasty surprises waiting to come out of the woodwork, at least put a red flag on the visual management and take some action.' He ran a hand over his face. 'I have to report to Ed at four o'clock. I suggest we all get back to work and I hope we all still have jobs after this fiasco.'

***

At four o'clock on the dot, Paul knocked on Ed's office door.

'Come in, Paul.'

Paul took a deep breath and walked straight in. He took a seat and felt his heart beating hard in his chest.

'Thank you for being prompt,' said Ed, then he got straight down to business. 'As I said earlier, I appreciate the attempt you made to set up visual management. You still have two weeks left to do it properly and the challenge still stands as before. What I want to do right now is provide you with some coaching to help you improve. I'm going to ask you some questions and I want you to think very hard about the answers.'

Paul nodded, hoping he could answer Ed's questions.

'Paul, why did your visual management fail to flag up the problem before it happened?' Ed asked, and then remained silent, allowing Paul time to formulate an answer.

Paul sat frozen in his chair, unsure what to say. He didn't feel it appropriate to go through all the excuses his team had given him – that would only dig a deeper hole for him to have to climb out of. The silence started to feel painful and he finally blurted out, 'I tried to implement visual management, but it didn't work.'

'Why do you think that was?'

'I allowed my team to choose the KPIs and they failed to choose the right ones.'

Ed nodded. 'That's a good start, Paul. Why did your team choose the wrong KPIs?'

Paul considered the question and took a full twenty seconds to formulate his thoughts.

'I think there are three reasons,' he said eventually. 'They didn't give it their best shot because they don't appreciate the benefits of visual management. They put in the minimum effort.'

'And?'

'I didn't check the visual management carefully enough to make sure that it contained all necessary and sufficient KPIs.'

'And the third?'

'I believe that my team fear showing red "X"s on the KPIs that relate to their area of responsibility because they see it as failure that could get them into trouble.'

'Let's start with the first reason,' said Ed. 'Why didn't your team understand the benefits?'

'The honest answer,' said Paul, 'is because I don't fully understand the benefits myself. I should have asked Mariam Khan to explain them to me, but I was more focused on understanding what I needed to do to get visual management working.'

Ed thought for a while. 'I can help to put that right by giving you a list of benefits, but to be honest you'll only really believe it when you experience it for yourself. What about the second reason. Why didn't you check the visual management yourself to make sure that it contained all necessary and sufficient KPIs?'

Paul sat back in his chair, exhaled loudly and considered the question. 'I don't like to micromanage my people,' he said. 'I believe in delegation and I don't like to challenge their opinions because they have a higher level of knowledge of their departments than I do.'

'After what has happened today, do you still believe that's true?'

Paul paused. 'No,' he said. 'I need to understand how our systems work better – how processes interact. And maybe I do need to be more hands-on.'

'Where do you get your knowledge of what goes on in reality?'

'Mostly, from reports my team submit . I read them in my office every week. I also hold weekly meetings with my team where we talk through what has been happening during the previous week.'

'And there lies your problem,' said Ed. 'You're relying on secondary data rather than seeing the facts for yourself. You have become so remote that people will tell you what they think you want to hear. If you don't understand the reality of your business, how do you know which details you should be worrying about? From now on I suggest you forget the reports and start taking a real interest in what is really going on in your departments. I want you to understand how they work, how they interconnect as a system to deliver value, and what problems they are having. You'll only get this level of information by getting out of your office and going to see what is really going on. I need you to start walking the floor, open your eyes and start talking to people at all levels. I want you to build relationships and trust to make sure that you have a reliable reporting structure – so when there's a problem, you hear about it quickly. Visual management is a tool to help you do this. I want you to pin up a visual KPI chart in your office with a daily target of two hours a day out in the workplace. Every day I want you to tick off the number of hours you spend with your teams.'

'I agree that micromanagement is bad. But that doesn't mean that hands-off delegation is good. People have different levels of competency and you have a responsibility to check and follow up when you delegate. Managers need to coach and support, and not just run their departments on blind faith.'

'I conduct annual appraisals,' said Paul. 'I review what people have been doing at those.'

'Annually is not nearly often enough,' said Ed. 'As a general rule, I expect monthly sit down reviews with each of your directs and day-to-day coaching during your walkabouts. I believe in a policy of flag and follow up.' (Refer to Appendix 7.) 'Flag and follow up means that you need to make clear what you want, empower people to do it and then follow up to see that they are doing it. You need to keep written notes otherwise you'll forget.

'The third reason you identified is a good point. Because of the way they have been treated in the past, employees often fear reporting bad news and problems. As leaders we need to change this by changing ourselves. One of the most important aspects of visual management is how people are treated when it is used. If people are treated badly when targets are missed, they'll resent the system and the leader. Leaders need to be process-focused – targets are missed because of bad processes, not bad people. This is a mindset change.

'A red "X" is not bad, as I'm sure Mariam already explained. A red "X" gives us the opportunity to put in place a fix or to change course in order to improve performance. You will need to explain this to your team, Paul, and then make sure you behave in the right way when the red "X"s start to appear. You need to be tough on the problems, but understanding of your people, just as I am being with you right now.'

Paul nodded.

'This leads naturally to the role of the leader as a coach to challenge and support people to solve problems and improve processes – turning the triangle upside down.' (Refer to Appendix 5.) 'To start with people may push back and be resistant, and this is natural because they are being asked to move out of their comfort zone. However, this is good for people and helps them grow and develop their abilities. Let me give you an example.

'Some years back I was asked to be best man at a friend's wedding. I felt it was an honour to be asked and not something that I could turn down, but then the reality began to sink in. Being best man carried with it a lot of responsibility – it wasn't just a case of making sure the groom and I turned up on time. I began to feel stressed, I tormented myself with the "what if?"s of the situation until I drove myself to distraction. And the thing I was most fearful of was the speech. At that time I'd barely ever spoken in front of an audience before. The wedding was a big, formal do, there was no getting out of it and every eye would be on me. I'd have done almost anything to get out of it – anything but let my friend down.

'So, despite my fears, I had to do it … and I did. I took time to write the best speech I could, and I practised and practised until I was word perfect. And do you know what? Afterwards, I felt fantastic. I had developed myself and really achieved something.'

Ed opened a desk drawer and drew out a small book. He slid it over the desk towards Paul. 'This is the new management handbook,' he said. 'I want you to read it as a matter of urgency and get to grips with the model of management expected by this company. I mentioned it earlier; it's called Turning The Triangle Upside Down. You'll also find a description of visual management and a list of the benefits it provides. I'll have a copy sent to each of your managers. Please make sure they read them.

'I'd also like you to go and see Mike Bailey, one of Mariam Khan's colleagues. Mike will help you understand the solutions to the problems we've been discussing today.'

Paul nodded, picked up the book and started to rise from his chair, ready to leave.

Ed held up his hand. 'Before you go, Paul, I'd like you to summarise the learning you've taken from our discussion today, and tell me what you'll do as a result.'

Paul quickly summarised the conversation and the learning points. 'As to actions,' he said, 'I'll set up a KPI chart for getting out into the work environment to improve my understanding, set up monthly reviews with each of my heads of department and take steps to become much more hands-on as a manager from now on. I'll also set up a meeting with Mike Bailey in the next couple of days.'

Ed sat patiently making notes in his leather notebook as Paul described the actions he would carry out. When he was finished, Ed said with a wry smile, 'I'll also schedule you in for a monthly review meeting with me, Paul. Assuming you're still with us, that is.'

Chapter 5

Paul under pressure

Back in his office, Paul reflected on what Ed had told him. While it made sense, it was still proving tricky to get to grips with. Mariam Khan's display had been easy to follow and all made sense, but of course its value depended on the quality of the information it was based on. That's why his had been a joke. He remembered how smug he'd felt when he showed the visual display – with all its comforting, trouble-free green 'O's – to Ed, and how the customer email Ed handed him had burst his bubble of complacency.

He sighed, picked up the phone, and put in a call to Mike Bailey.

'Of course – come in the morning,' said Mike, 'I'll be happy to share what I know about visual management with you. See you then!'

The management handbook Ed had given him sat on the desk, and Paul eyed it suspiciously. He supposed he'd have to find time to read it, but he didn't feel very enthusiastic. It seemed like a lot of effort to go to for a job he might no longer have in two weeks' time.

He went into the meeting room, grabbed some coloured pens, turned to a clean page on the flip chart pad and drew up a basic KPI chart for the time he aimed to spend in the workplace. Satisfied that what he'd done might be rough and ready, but was clearly understandable, he ripped the sheet from the pad and went back to his office, where he stuck it on the wall.

Next he composed an email to his heads of department explaining that he was going to be spending more time on the 'shop floor' and also implementing monthly reviews, starting the first week of the following month. 'Assuming I'm still here, anyway,' he muttered, as he clicked 'send'. He wondered if they'd raise their hackles against monthly reviews the way they were pushing back against visual management. He hoped the list of benefits Ed had promised to circulate would help oil the wheels of cooperation. (Refer to Appendix 8.)

That done, Paul decided to call it a day; he grabbed his jacket and his satchel and headed down to the car.

At home things were no better. As soon as he was in the door, Rebecca started waving brochures and talking about nursing homes. He plonked down at the kitchen table, nodding and agreeing in what he hoped were the right places, his mind still on his problems at work, then heard his wife say, 'Good, that's sorted, then.'

'What?' he said, realising too late that he had agreed to something he might well regret.

'The visits, this weekend.'

Paul looked blank.

'To the nursing homes, for Mum!' she said, exasperated. 'I'll set them up so we visit the top three on Saturday, then we can make a decision.'

'Visit three nursing homes? How long will that take?'

'A few hours. Why, have you got something better to do than to find a safe place to live for the woman who babysat your kids without a murmur of complaint, picked them up from school and cooked more meals for them than I can count?'

'No, of course not. It's just that—'

'Just that what? You'd rather watch the match or go to the pub?'

Paul said nothing; he'd had both on his agenda, but he knew now wasn't the time to say so. 'Anyway, how much are these nursing homes going to cost?' he asked.

'I knew you weren't listening! Here.' Rebecca threw some brochures and a sheet of paper with notes and figures on it onto the table. 'See for yourself.'

Paul glanced at the figures and gave a low whistle.

'Don't you dare say we can't afford it!' said Rebecca. 'After everything she's done for us …'

'I didn't … I'm not …' Paul protested, but his face gave him away.

'I'm going out,' said Rebecca, and she picked up her bag and headed for the door, snagging her jacket from the banister as she passed.

'Where? How long will you be?'

The answer was a slammed door. The house was silent after she'd left and Paul sat back in the chair and sighed. He looked at the figures again; it wasn't that he minded the cost, he was just afraid he wouldn't have a salary coming in to pay the fees with. Sure, he'd likely get a decent severance package, but where would he get another job, at his age? The market was tough. He couldn't tell Rebecca, though; she had enough on her plate. He just hoped that Mike Bailey would have some insights for him in the morning.

Chapter 6

Visual management process confirmation

The following morning Paul left home later than usual. A couple of weeks earlier he had received a letter asking him to attend an appointment at his local doctor's surgery for a health check, and today was the day. He had arranged to meet Mike at 10 a.m., giving himself plenty of time to attend the appointment.

After a short spell in the waiting room he was instructed to make his way through to his doctor's surgery. Paul knocked on the door and was invited to come in.

'Good morning, Mr Wayman. Please take a seat,' said the young Asian doctor. 'I see you are here for a health check. Thank you for attending; we recommend that people of your age undertake these checks every ten years.'

Paul sat down; he felt a little nervous, he really didn't like getting poked and prodded by doctors. 'What does it entail?' he asked.

'I'd like to check your cholesterol level, your blood pressure, and also to weigh you,' said the doctor. 'It won't take very long. I'll start by checking your blood pressure. Please roll up your shirt sleeve on your right arm?'

The doctor began uncoiling his blood pressure monitor. Paul watched as the doctor slid the cuff onto his arm, adjusted its position and then started inflating it by repeatedly squeezing the rubber bulb. The cuff became very tight and Paul could feel the pulse in his arm. The doctor released the air and made a note on his pad.

'Hmm,' he said. 'Your blood pressure is a little too high.'

'Is that bad?'

'Well, it's putting a strain on your heart and that increases your risk of having a heart attack or a stroke.'

'That's not a good result, then,' said Paul, feeling anxious.

'No, but we can do something about it. We measure and respond to blood pressure so that we reduce the risk of a very bad result.'

'What can I do to reduce the risk?'

'I advise you to buy your own blood pressure monitor,' said the doctor, 'and start monitoring your blood pressure each week. I also want you to monitor your salt intake, your exercise and your alcohol intake. Your target is a maximum of six grammes of salt per day, a minimum of half an hour's exercise on four days per week, and no more than twenty units of alcohol per week. Keep to that, and your blood pressure should fall back to safe levels. I want you to come in and see me again in one month. Hopefully that will do the trick and we'll not need to take any further action.'

The doctor proceeded to carry out the other tests and in all other respects, Paul was declared fit and healthy.

Paul headed back to reception and booked a second appointment for a month's time, then walked out to his car. *No wonder my blood pressure's up*, he thought, *with all the stress at work and at home, it would be a miracle if it wasn't.*

The previous evening Rebecca had come home full of apologies for flying off the handle and Paul had said sorry for not paying attention to her, but he still hadn't explained about the situation at work. While driving to meet Mike Bailey, he reflected on his experience with the doctor.

Maybe there are some similarities between this and my situation at work, he thought. *The doctor said I can avoid the risk of a heart attack by monitoring and controlling my salt and alcohol intake, and by ensuring I achieve a target level of exercise. At work I want to avoid the risk of delivering my services late and paying penalties. The question is, what are the results I need to monitor to avoid those risks?*

After a short journey, Paul drove through the now familiar gates, parked his car and made his way inside. As the reception area was unattended, he followed Mike's instructions and took the lift to the second floor. He exited and walked through some double doors into a corridor. After walking a short distance he found Mike Bailey's office; the door was open. Inside, an elderly gentleman, tall and very well dressed, was just putting on his jacket. As the man turned he was startled by Paul's presence.

'Oh, my goodness,' he said, 'you made me jump.'

'I'm sorry. I'm Paul Wayman, we spoke on the phone.'

'Ah, yes of course. I'm Mike.' They shook hands. 'I'm actually just on my way out of the office and it would be good if you could accompany me. Before we go, though, I'd like you to bring me up to speed with your situation. Please, have a seat.'

Mike pulled out a chair for Paul and returned to his own at the other side of the desk. 'Tell me what you know so far about visual management.'

Paul gave Mike a quick summary of his learning from Mariam and from

Ed.

Mike listened intently, then said, 'Tell me what progress you have made so far.'

Paul summarised his activities over the week and finished by describing his frustration with his team.

Mike chuckled. 'Don't worry,' he said, 'the problems you've encountered are a good opportunity to learn.'

'I've already received some coaching from Ed.'

'That's good,' said Mike. 'So how can I help?'

'Two questions,' said Paul. 'Where did my team go wrong with their KPIs? And how do I learn the right behaviours and mindset that Ed keeps talking about?'

'Let's start with the first question; where did you and your team go wrong with your KPIs?' said Mike. 'The first thing you need to ask is what are the results that you need to demonstrate to Ed?'

Mike looked expectantly at Paul over the top of his glasses.

'I need to demonstrate all results that are both necessary and sufficient,' said Paul.

'Good,' said Mike. 'And what are they?'

'Ultimately, I think Ed wants me to demonstrate a healthy profit, a good return on investment, and a healthy cash flow. I also need to keep my customers happy and be safe in all operations.'

'Okay,' said Mike, 'they are the top level results you need to show. Can you easily measure those results operationally on a daily or weekly basis?'

'We can measure safety directly by measuring accidents and near misses, but it's not so easy to measure customer satisfaction, profit, and cash flow operationally. I think it would be easier to measure weekly on-time service delivery, productivity efficiency, right-first-time quality, and costs. These results ultimately convert into customer satisfaction and profit.'

'There you are, then,' said Mike, smiling. 'You've identified the top level results that you can measure on a weekly basis. That's the first discussion you need to have with your team. You should also speak to Ed and ask him what his strategic objectives are, because you need to make sure that your top level results are fully aligned with those. Understanding Ed's strategic objectives will also help you to identify the operational target levels you need to set to meet Ed's expectations.'

'That's a good point,' said Paul. 'I don't think Ed accepts our current target levels.'

'So, Paul, does that answer your question of where you went wrong with your KPIs?'

'No ... not really,' said Paul. 'The thing is, I think we already have most of those KPIs on our visual display. We probably don't have the right targets, but even if we did, it wouldn't have helped stop the problem we experienced.'

Mike nodded. 'Unfortunately, identifying and monitoring all necessary and sufficient top-level results is not enough to ensure you get good results in practice.'

Paul frowned, nodded, and continued to listen to Mike.

'Have you heard of "lead and lag KPIs"?' (Refer to Appendix 9.)

Paul shook his head.

'You can look up their definition in your management handbook, but I'll give you a quick summary.'

Mike stood up and turned to the flip chart, where he wrote:

Lag KPI = results indicator (reactive)
Lead KPI = system performance indicator (reactive or proactive)

'There's also a special type of leading KPI called the activity KPI,' said Mike. "These are Proactive KPIs.

'To have a successful visual management process, you need the right balance of these three types of KPI. The KPIs you have just identified are all lag KPIs. To reduce the risk of red "X"s on your lag KPIs, you need to monitor lead KPIs. Lead KPIs are the predictors of the lag KPIs.

'Put it another way. If you neglect your lead KPIs then your lag KPIs will turn out bad. By monitoring lead KPIs and taking timely action, you can protect the lag KPIs and hence the results.'

Paul was suddenly excited. 'That's just like my blood pressure,' he said.

Mike gave Paul a quizzical look.

Paul explained how he'd just been to see the doctor and had found out that his blood pressure was too high.

'The result I want,' said Paul, 'is to be healthy and free from the risk of a heart attack or stroke. That is my lag KPI. My blood pressure is a lead KPI. My salt intake, my alcohol intake and my level of exercise are all lead KPIs.'

'That's a great example. 'Your exercise level is also a good example of an activity KPI, because by proactively engaging in this activity you can positively influence the result.'

'Yes, I see.'

'The next thing you need to learn about is the KPI tree,' said Mike. (Refer to Figures 9, 9a and 9b, and Appendix 11.)

THE VISUAL MANAGER

KPI TREE

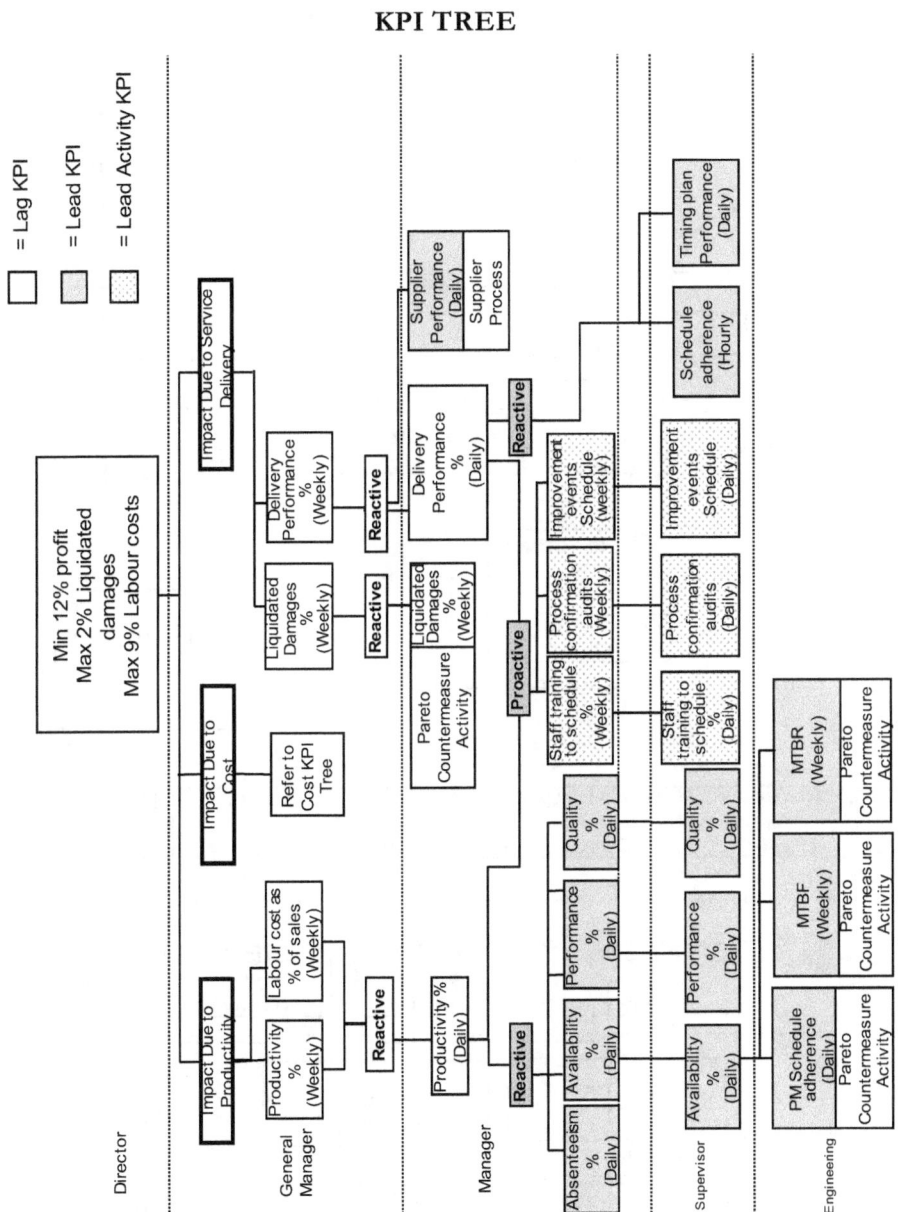

FIGURE 9

KPI TREE DETAIL 1

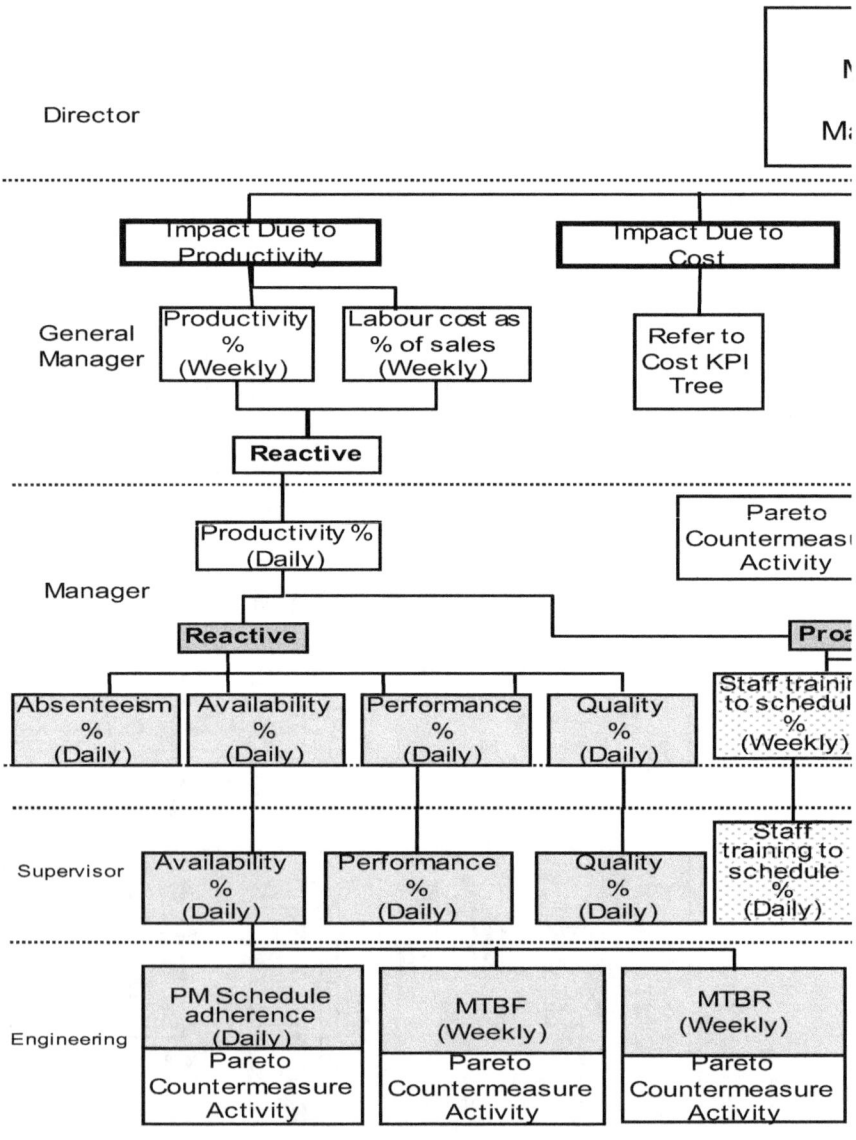

FIGURE 9a

KPI TREE DETAIL 2

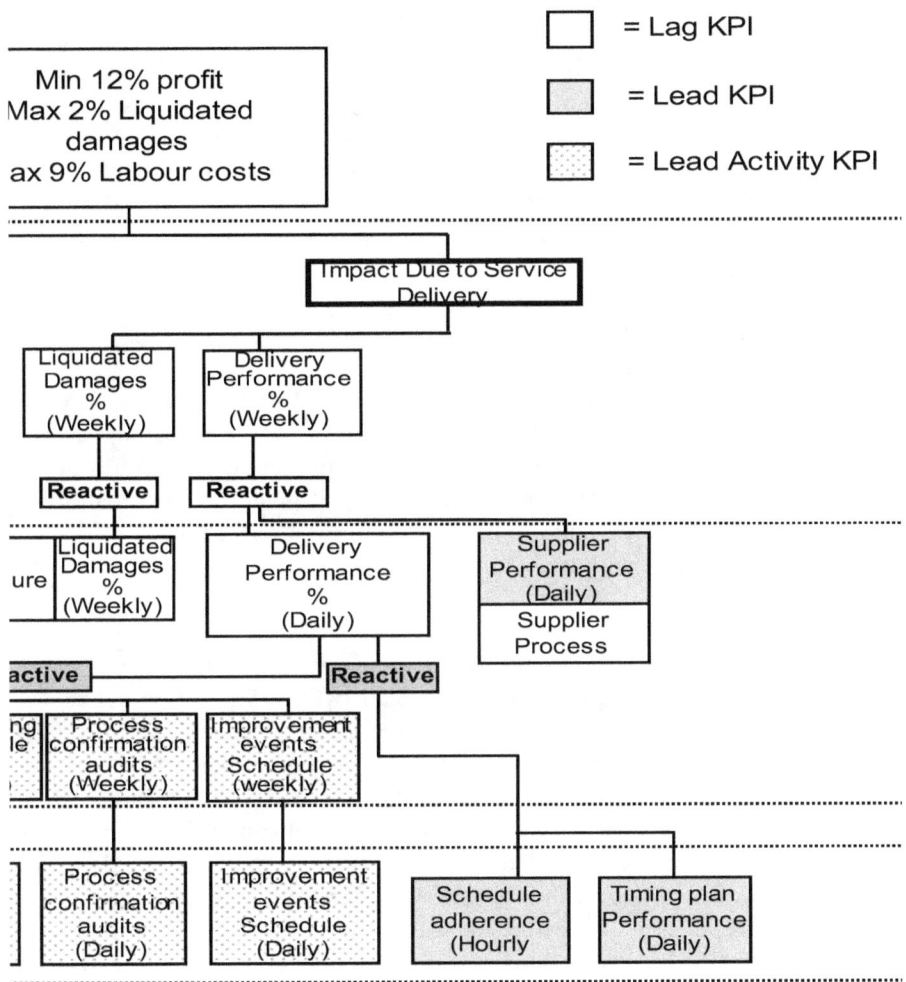

FIGURE 9b

'I've never heard of a KPI tree,' said Paul.

'It's a graphical method that helps you identify the right balance of lead and lag KPIs. It also shows the organisational level at which they should be measured, the targets, and the frequency at which they should be measured. You can look it up in your company handbook,' said Mike. 'It's a really good coaching tool. I recommend you lead a workshop and help your team draw out the KPI tree. You don't need to worry about trying to make it perfect, because you'll modify it as you gain more experience from actually using visual management in the future. Give it a try and give me call if you have any problems or questions.'

'Thanks, Mike,' said Paul, 'I'll do that.'

'Right,' said Mike. 'Let's now consider your second question, about behaviours and mindset.

'I'll teach you some of the behaviours to make it work successfully. In order for me to teach you what you need to know, we need to take a walk together. I'm going to show you how to conduct process confirmation of the visual display.' (Refer to Appendix 10.) 'This will give you information to help you coach your team, and is a key behaviour in its own right.

'Ready to take a walk with me, Paul?'

'Yes, of course.'

'Okay, then, let's go.'

They walked together down the corridor, turned right through a set of double doors, then entered a large open-plan office. There was a buzz of activity – many people were sitting together at small round tables, tightly engaged in discussions. Few people looked up as they walked past. Paul saw small teams of people gathered around flip charts. They appeared to be brainstorming and capturing ideas. Mike continued through the office to the far wall, where Paul recognised the now familiar layout of a display. The display was similar in appearance to the one Mariam had shown him on his previous visit. The KPI charts were measuring different things, but the layout was very similar and it used status at a glance and Pareto charts. Instead of three accountable areas, there were five: Purchasing, R&D, Technical Project Development, Safety and Design. Only R&D had a green 'O' at the top.

Mike stood back to take in an overview of the visual display. 'In an hour's time,' he began, continuing to study the display, 'there will be a visual review meeting. At this meeting I will lead a review of this display with my department heads.' He looked at Paul to see if he was paying attention, and was pleased to see he was listening attentively.

'I lead this review every week at ten thirty on Tuesday morning. My heads of department, whom you can see named, with their deputies, at the top of the visual display, are tasked with updating the visual display before 10 a.m. each Tuesday. This gives me a chance to review the visual display before the meeting. This is my process confirmation; my chance to quickly evaluate the visual display on my own and identify key questions that I wish to ask at the visual review meeting.'

As Paul was now familiar with the process of status at a glance, he too looked over the display and considered what he saw using the one, three, ten process.

Mike moved in closer to study some of the charts. He focused most attention on the ones with the Red 'X's and proceeded to make some notes in a small notebook.

'Can you explain what you are looking for and making notes about?' asked Paul.

'The first thing I'm doing,' said Mike, 'is testing for one, three, ten. I'm glad to say that this visual display passes that test.'

'What would you do if it didn't?'

'If it ever fails, then I'll speak to my accountable team members to coach them back to the acceptable standard.

'The second thing I'm looking for are problems or risks identified by the visual display that I am either not aware of or that do not appear to be getting solved.

'Take a look at this chart here, Paul.' Mike pointed to a KPI chart and Paul moved closer to study it. 'What do you see?'

'There's a red "X" in the corner, so the target for last week was not achieved,' said Paul.

'Good,' said Mike. 'Now tell me what else you can see and what questions you have.'

'I can see the main reason for last week's failure to hit target was a transport delay,' said Paul. 'And I can see from the Pareto chart that "transport delay" is the main reason for all the missed targets since the start of the year.'

'Very good,' said Mike. 'Does anything concern you about what you see on the chart?'

'I'm concerned that the target has been missed for the last four weeks,' said Paul. 'It doesn't look like performance is getting any better. I'm asking myself, what are the implications of this target being missed, and why is the problem of delayed transport not getting solved?'

'Very good,' said Mike. 'Those are my thoughts, also. I'll be asking questions at the review to find out what is going on and what steps are being taken to identify the root cause. I'll also be looking to see what support I might need to give to help my team remedy the situation.'

'The third thing I am looking for is adherence to standard.' Mike pointed to a chart on the finance visual display. 'I need to do some coaching around this one,' he said. 'This chart is not up to the standard that is expected.'

'What do you mean?'

'There is no target line on this chart. Didn't Mariam Khan tell you the minimum standards expected for a KPI chart?'

Paul shook his head. 'No, she didn't have time.'

Mike pointed to a picture to the far right of the visual display. Paul walked over and studied it.

'Each KPI chart must satisfy the standard given on that picture,' said Mike. (Refer to Figure 10.)

'When I come and review the visual display, I am also looking to confirm that standards are not slipping. If I see that, I'll work to ensure that they're re-established.'

'So that means that standards must be defined so that everyone knows what they are, right?' asked Paul.

STANDARDISED VISUAL MANAGEMENT CHART

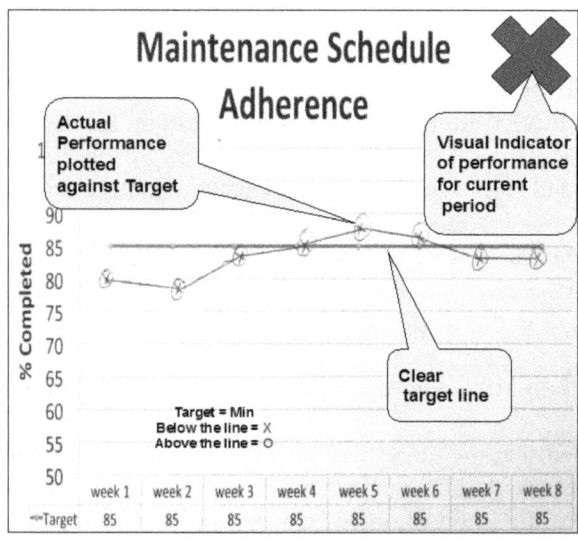

FIGURE 10

'Correct. To clearly define standards and make them visible in words and pictures – that's key.'

'Could I take a photo of that standard?' asked Paul.

'Yes, of course', said Mike, 'photograph all you like. I'm a firm believer in stealing with pride.'

Paul took out his mobile phone and proceeded to take several photos.

'The last thing I look for when I carry out process confirmation is team and leadership alignment.' Mike turned to look at Paul. 'Visual management helps a leader test their vision of what is important against the team's vision of what is important.'

'I'm not sure I understand you.'

'Let me explain. When you challenge your own team to set up their visual display, you'll coach them to do it, but not do it for them, right?'

'Yes,' said Paul, 'I tend to use that approach.'

'Good,' said Mike. 'The management mindset in this organisation is to coach and not fix. That means you will challenge and coach your team to do it, but not do it for them. If you do it for them, they will neither learn from the experience nor will they feel they own what has been produced.'

'Okay, I get the idea,' said Paul. 'I'm glad I took the right approach, then, even though it didn't turn out so well.'

'When you first coach your team to set up their visual display you'll go through a coaching process that will result in an agreed KPI tree. This KPI tree will be good enough to start the visual management process. The issue,' said Mike, 'is that all businesses are dynamic and that means the KPI tree will need to change over time to remain effective. As a leader you need to keep testing the visual display against your understanding of the current business situation and verify that it is still good enough. What you will find is that your team will often have a different view of what is important from what you see as important. This provides for important coaching conversations with your team and helps you stay aligned.'

Paul still looked puzzled. 'Can you give me an example?' he asked.

'Certainly,' said Mike. 'I know from my involvement with the purchasing department that they are involved with a big new construction project. This construction project is being project managed by us for one of our major customers and is worth many millions of pounds. This project requires specialist materials from several different countries. The timeliness of these materials will mean the difference between the success or failure of this project. I want to see some visual control around the status and timeliness of these materials. I want to see a KPI chart or a visual schedule tracking the timely ordering, manufacture and delivery of the materials. This information is not on the visual display and I want to see it displayed. I want to see this information because I have had bad experiences with specialist material delays in the past. I have considerably more experience than my team in this area and I know that problems can occur and need to be sorted out very quickly before they turn into a disaster.'

'I think I now get it,' said Paul. 'The visual display allows you to see the things that your team believe are the most important things to measure. Sometimes the team won't recognise certain risks that need to be monitored or don't have the experience to judge what the biggest risks are. The leader needs to check what the team is measuring and test it against his own understanding and experience.'

'Precisely,' said Mike. 'Sometimes the team will be measuring too many things, not enough things, or the wrong things, and you need to re-align them using your experience and expectations. A trap I see many leaders fall into is assuming their team sees things the same way that they see them. This does not mean that the leader is always right when there is a visible misalignment, but it does at least drive a healthy and meaningful discussion.'

Mike continued to look at the charts and make notes. After he was finished, he took out a pen and wrote his initials and the date on each of the KPI charts.

'Why do you do that?' asked Paul.

'This is called "footprint management",' said Mike. 'By adding my initials and the date to the charts, I communicate that I have been here and carried out process confirmation. This sends out a powerful message to the whole team because it communicates that this visual information is important to me. The whole department can now see that their director has been here and paid attention to their visual display. This process also helps me, because each time I sign a chart I ask myself the question, am I satisfied with this chart? This makes me focus and pay attention to each one. Also, when Ed walks around this office, and he walks around a lot, I might add, he is also able to see that I have been paying attention to the visual display. Ed likes to see that his managers are hands on with their teams and that they lead by example. Leading by example means that our management behaviour reflects our words. Therefore, if I tell my team that visual management is important, I have to behave in a way that demonstrates my own commitment to it.'

'Does Ed walk around and look at all the visual displays?' asked Paul.

'Oh, yes. Ed believes in managing by walking about and he touches every single visual display in each company at least once per month.' Mike pointed to the top right hand corner of the visual display. 'That's Ed's footprint right there.' The initials 'E.B.' were clearly visible. 'Ed looks to confirm standards, of course, but he also looks for common problems and interdependencies across the visual displays in different areas of the organisation. He also believes in delegating the outcome, not the process.'

Paul nodded as realisation dawned. 'That's what he's doing to me now, isn't it?'

Mike chuckled. 'You're catching on.'

'How long did it take you to catch on?'

'Well, let's see … the old company was taken over two years ago and I was made a director eighteen months ago.'

'You were a manager in the old company?'

'That's right, Mariam Khan and I both were. We were prepared to learn and to change, and we were both rewarded for it.'

'What about your other colleagues?'

'Moved on of their own free will or were fired.' Mike sighed. 'We all had the same chances, but you have to be prepared to put the work in to survive.'

Paul nodded; *just like me and my high blood pressure*, he thought.

'I'm hungry,' said Mike. 'Would you like to join me for lunch?'

'That would be very nice,' said Paul, 'thank you.'

They headed to the canteen together. The canteen was very busy and they each selected a sandwich with coffee to avoid the queues for the hot food.

After sitting down to eat, they were joined by several other people. The conversation drifted over to office politics and Paul remained silent, just listening and contenting himself with his sandwich. Mike received a call on his mobile phone and excused himself from the table. Paul finished his sandwich and then pulled out his notebook to capture his thoughts.

After he finished writing, Paul was filled with new enthusiasm and felt re-energised to start working with his team on visual management. He decided to set off back to the office as soon as he had finished his coffee. If Mike Bailey and Mariam Khan could learn new methods and techniques, so could he. He would adapt to survive, as far as both his job and his health were concerned.

***

Paul's notebook entry

VISUAL MANAGEMENT PROCESS CONFIRMATION

Visual Management Process Confirmation allows the leader to spend time on his or her own so as to review the display, following an update by the team but before the visual review meeting.

This allows the leader to:

a) Identify the key questions he wants to ask at the visual review meeting – e.g. Why is this KPI repeatedly off target? What is the impact? and, What do we need to do to get it back on target?

b) Check the standard of the visual management – for example, are the charts drawn to the correct standard? Has the display been updated in a timely manner and correctly? Does it meet the 1, 3, 10 standard?

c) Test the alignment between the leader and his team. Are the charts focused on tracking the same risks and priorities that the leader has in mind?

d) Use footprint management to sign and date the charts. This ensures the leader pays attention to each chart and communicates the importance to the team (and Ed) by showing that the leader is paying attention.

Chapter 7

Getting the team on board

The following morning, Wednesday of the week after his first meeting with Ed, Paul was standing at the whiteboard of the conference centre meeting room. The 18th century hall, nestling in three hundred and fifty acres of landscaped parkland, provided for an impressive setting. The room, formerly a bedroom, was bright, flooded with sunlight, and overlooking a lake. The walls and ceiling were panelled in oak and adorned with paintings and woodcarvings. Although expensive, Paul felt the venue was worth it; nothing was more important right now than ensuring his team's undivided attention to the task at hand. This was make or break.

Sarah, Peter, Helen and Brian looked sceptical as Paul explained how he wanted them all to work together to create a KPI tree (refer to Figure 9 and Appendix 11). He went through the need for both lead and lag KPIs (refer to Appendix 9) and told them the story of his visit to the doctor. He drew a diagram to illustrate how lead KPIs supported lag KPIs. Finally, he explained the need for clear standards and how process confirmation was required at all levels of management.

All of them were quiet until Paul finished his explanation. Finally, Helen spoke up. 'Where did you learn all of that?'

'Mike Bailey explained it all to me yesterday.'

'Who?' asked Brian.

'Mike Bailey?' asked Sarah.

'Yes,' said Paul, feeling defensive, but determined to press on.

'So now you are going to show us all how to do it, are you?' asked Peter.

'No,' replied Paul. 'I want you to do it yourselves, and I'll coach you, so let's get started. The first thing I want you to consider is this email I received from Ed Deacon just one hour ago.' Paul handed a copy to each person. 'As you can see by the title, these are the strategic objectives for the next twelve months.'

'These are tough targets!' said Helen. 'Zero accidents, no more than two per cent absence due to illness. Twelve per cent profit in the first year, with a maximum of two per cent liquidated damages, ten per cent improvement in customer loyalty, and a maximum nine per cent labour cost each month. And on top of that, Ed expects us to project manage the upgrade of the computer system and manage the change of our suppliers.'

'I know, it's tough,' said Paul. 'It's a big stretch from what we have achieved before; the question is, what does it mean in terms of our operational performance?'

Whilst Paul was talking, Sarah was busy scribbling some calculations on a notepad. She looked up. 'It means that we need to up our service delivery performance to ninety-eight per cent, improve our productivity by ten per cent, improve our right-first-time quality to ninety-nine per cent and reduce our costs by twelve per cent.'

Helen took the notepad and quickly looked through the calculations, then blew air through her lips in a soft whistle. 'We've only achieved that level of performance once in the last twenty-four months.'

'Do you feel it's possible to operate at that level of performance?' asked Paul.

'Anything is possible,' said Brian, joining in the conversation for the first time, 'but I don't feel very confident.'

'Can we negotiate with Ed?' asked Peter. 'There seems little point promising a level of performance we don't believe we can deliver.'

'We can try,' said Paul, 'but the feeling I get is that he will expect us to show that we have a plan to get to that level of performance, even if we can't deliver it right now. As you said, Helen, we have achieved that level of performance once in the last two years, so it is possible. We just need to find a way to replicate that level of performance every week.'

The room became quiet and Paul could feel the negativity. He decided to reveal the ace up his sleeve.

'To help us all feel a bit more positive, I've organised a little trip. I've arranged with Mike Bailey and Mariam Khan for them to give us a tour of their company.'

'When will we do that?' asked Helen.

'How about right now?' said Paul. 'I chose this conference centre because it's just around the corner from our new sister company. Mike Bailey and Mariam Khan have organised a special tour for us, focused around visual management. We won't get to attend a visual management meeting, but we will see lots of examples. We'll also have the opportunity to talk to people at various levels about how visual management has helped them.'

'How long is this going to take?' asked Helen. 'We've got a lot to get through today.'

'Yes, we have, but the trip will only take a couple of hours. We'll come back here afterwards and continue our work.' He shook his car keys. 'Come on, I'll drive.'

***

The visit was a great success. Mike and Mariam gave the team a full tour of the company. They explained how visual management worked, and what they had achieved in terms of results and benefits. They encouraged Paul's team to talk to employees at all levels about visual management and how they felt about it. Mariam had organised a talk from an operations manager and her supervisor. They explained how red 'X's were used to drive improvement and not seen as negative or as a poor reflection on the accountable individual. The supervisor explained how improvement workshops were scheduled each year to target specific processes and rapidly drive up performance – these were always led by the head of department. (Refer to Appendix 12.) Finally Mike took the team to an empty office where he showed them an example of the original KPI tree constructed out of brown paper and Post-it notes. The scepticism of Paul's team gradually melted away, everyone thoroughly enjoyed the trip, and the team headed back to the conference centre feeling much more positive than when they'd left.

***

'Right, we need to do some work now,' Paul said. They were back in the meeting room, and he had the floor. 'I'm going to set you a task and I want you all to work on it together whilst I go and get us some tea and coffee. When I come back, I'd like you to present your recommendations to me.'

While his team exchanged glances, Paul delved into his leather satchel and pulled out a pile of management handbooks, which he placed on the table.

'Here you go, these will help,' he said. 'There's a great description of the KPI tree in the management handbook. It explains the idea better than I did earlier and you'll need to understand it fully to complete the challenge I'm going to set you.'

Paul walked over to the white board and started to write.

What should the basic structure of our KPI tree look like?

'There you are,' said Paul. 'I want you to discuss this question and formulate a response. There are no right or wrong answers. When I come back, I'd like you to present your proposal to me.'

Brian, Helen, Peter and Sarah gave each other blank looks.

Paul pushed the top of the dry-wipe marker back onto the pen with an audible snap. 'I'll see you in twenty minutes,' he said, and left the room.

***

When Paul returned he was carrying a silver tray piled high with biscuits, cakes, cups, tea, and coffee. He pushed the heavy oak door open with his foot and was greeted by a buzz of activity. All four members of his team were on their feet and drawing a diagram on the white board. Paul set the tray on the table and sat down, not wanting to disturb the positive activity that was taking place. After ten minutes, everyone returned to their seats and Paul began to distribute tea and coffee.

'Wow,' said Paul, nibbling a biscuit. 'It certainly looks like you've been very busy. Could you talk me through what you have come up with?'

Brian stood up and walked up to the white board.

'The first issue we discussed,' he said, 'is how can we effectively protect lag KPIs by focusing on lead KPIs. As you said, Paul, in order to improve your blood pressure by the time of your next doctor's appointment, you need to monitor and control your salt and alcohol intake, and exercise on a daily basis.'

Brian paused and looked at Paul to see if he was on the right track. Paul nodded. 'Keep going, he said, 'I'm intrigued.'

'As managers,' said Brian, 'we are not in the best position to monitor lead KPIs and react to them on a high frequency basis. We propose that we get our supervisors and team members involved with visual management and help them set up daily visual management to monitor and control lead KPIs. We'll coach them to review their visual management daily and take action to correct lead KPIs that are off target.'

'That makes sense,' said Paul. 'By involving the supervisors and team members we'll be increasing the number of people solving problems.'

'Exactly,' said Brian, 'and where they can't solve their problems, they'll escalate to us.'

'Actually,' said Helen, 'we thought it a good idea that we go along and attend their visual management meetings two or three times per week. By doing that we can see what problems they're having and get involved to support them.'

'Therefore, we need two levels of visual management,' said Paul. 'Daily for the supervisors and weekly for us.'

'Two levels is fine for Peter, Helen and Brian,' said Sarah, 'but I need three levels because I have six supervisors, each supporting ten to fifteen team members.' (Refer to Figure 11).

3 LEVELS OF VISUAL MANAGEMENT (SARAH – OPERATIONS)

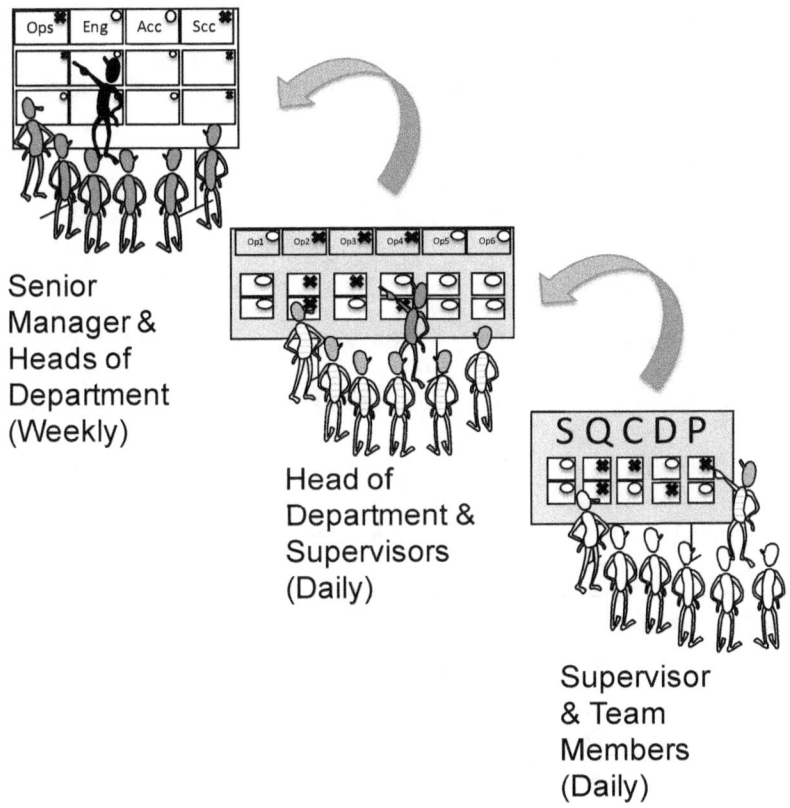

FIGURE 11

'I propose that each supervisor should hold a short daily visual management meeting with his or her team during the early morning. Supervisors will each have their own visual display. I'll then run a visual management meeting with all of my supervisors in the early afternoon using a central visual display summarising the information from the six lower level visual displays. This will drive three levels of problem-solving against targets each week. Level one, daily with the supervisors and their teams; level two, daily, with my supervisors and me; level three, weekly with us and you, Paul.'

'That's a great idea,' said Paul. 'I love how we are getting more people involved. Focusing on daily actions should speed up the problem-solving process and help lag KPIs stay on target.

'I accept your proposal and I'd like each of you to think about an implementation plan for setting up your visual displays and for starting the visual management meetings on a daily basis with your supervisors.'

Paul paused. 'I'd now like us to start identifying the lead and lag KPIs that we need. I propose we make a start with safety. Peter, would you please write your current measures for safety on the white board.'

Peter got up and walked to the front. He picked up a pen and wrote on the white board:

- *Accidents – lost time and minor*
- *Near misses*

'This is currently all I measure,' he said, 'and I'm not sure how I can improve them.'

'Okay,' said Paul. 'Who can offer suggestions for how Peter can improve his KPIs?'

'Before we do that,' said Helen, 'I suggest that Peter writes the top level objectives above his KPIs.'

Peter nodded and drew a box above the two KPIs. In the box he wrote two targets.

- *Zero accidents*
- *Max 2% lost time due to illness or work related issues*

'Next,' said Brian, 'we need to identify the different ways these targets could be adversely impacted.'

'I'm unclear what you mean,' said Peter. 'Can you help me out, Brian?' He held out the pen.

Brian jumped up, walked to the white board and took the pen.

Beneath the target box he drew three more boxes.

Impact due to accident	*Impact due to work-related issue – e.g. repetitive strain*	*Impact due to illness*

'Ah, now I understand,' said Peter, 'I need to make sure my lag KPIs can measure each of these three impacting conditions. It appears accidents and near misses only fit under the "Impact due to accident" box. I need lag KPIs for the other two conditions.' He turned to the white board and started to write.

- *Lost time due to absence or reduced work ability – target TBA*

'This will measure the impact due to work related issues. I now need to add one final lag KPI.' He turned back to the board.

- *Lost time due to illness – target TBA*

'I think these lag KPIs should be measured both weekly on our visual display and daily at the supervisor level.'

Peter turned to face the others. 'I now need some leading KPIs,' he said. 'Any ideas?'

'I have an idea,' said Sarah. 'I think we need to carry out field visits and inspections of our processes. I believe that many accidents and near misses could be avoided if we were prepared to look closely at our processes and ask our people their opinions on risks.'

'Okay,' said Peter, 'I could plan to target a check and inspect audit on a fixed number of processes each day.' He wrote down the idea on the board.

'I think we need to add safety training as a lead KPI,' said Brian.

Peter wrote it down.

'I have one,' said Helen. 'I've worked on some of our processes and after only one day I had backache. I think we need to carry out audits on posture confirmation.'

'That's a really good lead KPI for impact due to work-related issues,' said Peter.

The team continued to discuss and brainstorm the lead KPIs. Within ten minutes they produced a list.

- *Field visits and process inspections – target number per day (proactive)*
- *Unsafe conditions reported – target TBA (reactive)*
- *Safety training – targeted to schedule: 100% (proactive)*
- *Posture confirmation checks – target number per day TBA (proactive)*
- *Pre-employment medical check – target = every new employee: 100% (proactive)*
- *Return to work discussion – every time there is a lost time event: 100% (proactive)*

- *Process rotations – 3 rotations per team member per day, where viable: 90% (proactive)*

'That's a great list,' said Paul, 'and nearly all of those KPIs are proactive. Definitely an improvement on what we have already. I want you to go through them with your team and allow them to add their own ideas to expand the list. Also, how will we put these activities into practice? And at what level will they be measured and acted upon?'

'I'll talk to my safety team,' said Peter. 'I'll work with them to agree the list, and define the standards, accountabilities and the targets for each. I'll put it all together as a KPI tree.'

'Excellent,' said Paul. 'When will I be able to see your final list, standards, accountabilities and targets?'

Peter thought about it. 'I'll have them ready by Friday,' he said.

'Okay,' said Paul making a note. 'That's fine. I'd also like you to add a lead KPI on the countermeasure ratio. In other words, I'd like a KPI to show how many issues have been identified and how many have been solved. I'll leave it up to you and your team to propose a target percentage ratio for this.'

Peter nodded, adding the KPI to the list on the board.

'Peter, could you take a photograph of the board then wipe it clean, please? I'd like to move on and start looking at productivity and delivery performance.'

Peter used his mobile phone to take several photographs of the white board and then wiped it clean.

Paul turned and smiled at Sarah. 'Would you please take us through your KPIs, Sarah?' he said.

Sarah stood up and walked to the white board. She started by drawing a box, then entered the relevant top level targets for profit, liquidated damages and labour cost.

- *Min 12% profit*
- *Max 2% liquidated damages*
- *Max 9% labour cost*

She then drew two boxes below the first box.

Impact due to productivity

Impact due to scheduled service delivery

'I already have the lag KPIs in place for both of these,' she said, 'but they're currently only measured at my level. I propose to also measure them at supervisor level.'

Paul nodded and she continued.

'I'd like to now focus on productivity. I have some ideas for the lead KPIs for productivity and I'll write these down as a list on the board so you can see them. Some of these are already measured, but none of them are visual or have targets to drive improvement.' She wrote:

- *Absenteeism – target max of 3% (reactive)*
- *Staff training and competence validation – 100% delivery of scheduled improvement of skills (proactive)*
- *Facilities and equipment – %TBA available at the right time and correct speed (reactive)*
- *Process quality – 3% max defect output (reactive)*
- *Process audits – 100% schedule adherence (proactive)*

Paul took a hard look at the KPIs and said, 'What about supplier service performance; isn't that important to monitor and improve?'

Sarah though about it and then added it to the list.

- *Supplier service performance – timeliness and quality (% to be determined) (reactive)*

'Do you think we need more proactive KPIs?' asked Paul.

'I have an idea for a proactive KPI,' said Sarah. 'I'd like to add a KPI to track the delivery of six improvement events. As we've already discussed, I need to increase my productivity by a minimum of ten per cent in order to meet the profitability target. This will be very tough to both achieve and sustain. I have a way that I could progressively achieve improvements in efficiency, delivery performance and quality. I received a visit yesterday from Karl Fox. Karl is the new divisional head of business improvement. He offered me the support of his improvement team provided I allocate them to projects that demonstrate a strong business case and also take an active role in their delivery. I propose that I set a lead KPI for the delivery of six improvement projects. I'll use Pareto analysis to focus on the biggest issues and space the projects out throughout the year. The KPI will visibly track their timeliness and effectiveness, and I'll set a stepped productivity target line, in line with their delivery.' (Refer to Figure 12.)

'That's a fantastic proposal,' said Paul.

KPI CHART WITH STEPPED TARGET LINE

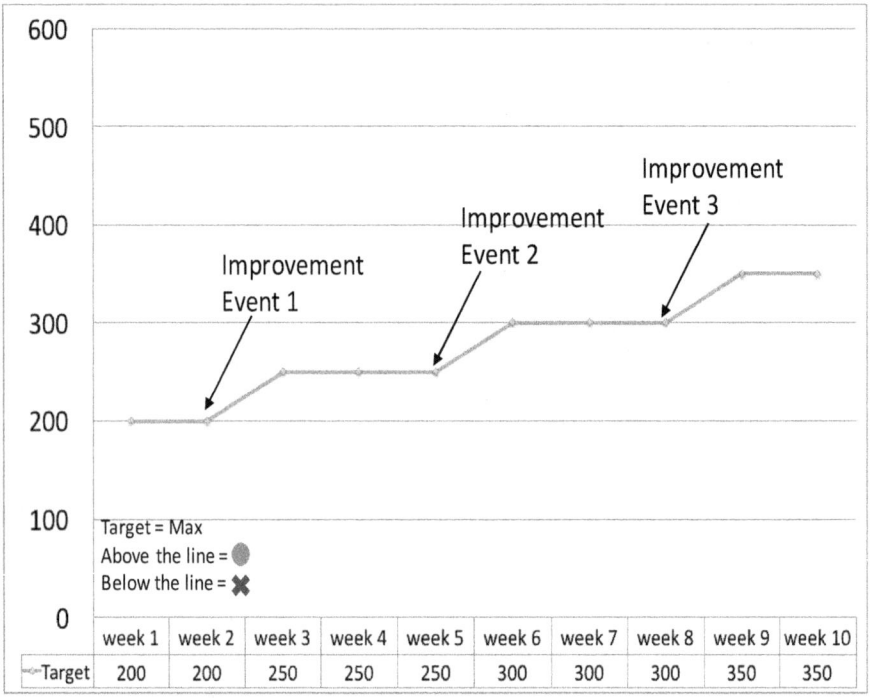

FIGURE 12

'I have a second idea to drive improvement,' said Sarah. 'I learned a new technique on the visit today. The operations manager, Phil Howard, showed me how they control their critical processes. I think it could help us achieve our targets. The technique is called short interval control.' (Refer to Figure 13 and Appendix 13.)

'I've never heard of it,' said Paul. He looked at the other members of the team and they shook their heads.

'Short interval control,' explained Sarah, 'works by monitoring selected processes at many intervals throughout the day. The results from the processes are visually recorded every hour. Every three hours a manager and the relevant supervisor go to the process and review the results. They agree rapid actions to get back on track, fix problems and re-stabilise the process. Phil told me that this alone raised his productivity by ten per cent. The interval can be adjusted from one hour up to four hours.'

THE VISUAL MANAGER

SHORT INTERVAL CONTROL BOARD

FIGURE 13

'I think that's a great idea,' said Paul. 'The idea fits with Ed's directive to get out of our offices and into the workplace.'

Helen put her hand up. 'Yes, Helen,' said Sarah.

'I'd like to add some KPIs that will support you, Sarah. You've identified facilities and equipment, and this falls under my area of accountability.'

Helen walked up to the white board and added a set of lead KPIs to support Sarah.

- Asset availability 95% (reactive)
- Preventative maintenance schedule adherence – 90% (reactive)
- Mean time to repair (reactive) – target TBA
- Mean time between failure (reactive) – target TBA

'These are KPIs I can use to drive my team's performance to support you,' said Helen. 'I'll need to calculate and agree my targets, but I can work this out and we can agree it together, if that's okay with you? I also need to be proactive, so in addition I'd like to plan in five improvement workshops this year. I'll set up a Pareto chart to identify the top five worst performing pieces of equipment and target the improvement projects on these. I'll track the projects just like you plan to, Sarah.'

'Fantastic,' said Paul, 'this is all coming together really well.'

Paul and his team continued to focus on identifying all lead and lag KPIs to satisfy the achievement of the top level targets. Within two hours they had identified all the KPIs they needed, the level at which they would be measured, and who would be accountable for their delivery.

Paul asked for commitments on identification of targets and for the production of charts to the standard defined in the management handbook, and recorded all commitments in his notebook.

By the end of the day everyone was tired, but happy with their accomplishments.

'I want to thank you all for a fantastic day's work,' said Paul. 'I have all your individual commitments and I ask you to honour these. Please work with your deputies and supervisors to work out both the targets and the practicalities for setting up the lower level visual management systems. If you have any problems, let me know how I can help support you. As before, we have the support of the two students, Stuart and Graham, for setting up the visual displays. I'll be scheduling meetings with each of you on Friday when you can update me on your charts, target lines and the commitments you have agreed with your supervisors. Thank you, and have a good evening.'

***

Over the next couple of days, Paul and his team worked tirelessly to set up their visual displays using the information generated during their KPI tree workshop. Mariam Khan and Mike Bailey extended their offer of a company tour to all the supervisors. Paul agreed that this needed to happen before any further moves were made to implement visual management at lower levels; the immediate priority was to set up their own visual management system.

Paul scheduled follow up meetings with each member of his team. He found to his delight that everyone honoured their commitments. However, setting the targets for the KPIs proved to be much trickier than Paul had anticipated.

The problem they faced was how to set and agree the targets so that they were neither too hard nor too easy. If the targets were set to be too easy, then they would not drive the need for improvement. On the other hand, if the targets were set to be too challenging, too soon, then they could be demotivating. As Sarah put it, 'If I don't feel it's possible to achieve a green KPI, then I'm likely to just accept my fate and not try too hard.'

Finally, Paul hit on a method that helped to achieve a balance. He asked his team to dig out the history of their performance and agreed to set the targets at the highest level achieved over the last six months. Many KPIs were also set up with target lines showing stepped improvement (refer to Figure 12). For each step up, Paul asked for a schedule of improvement workshops to drive the performance to a new level. He made it clear that his managers must lead these improvement workshops, although promised he would attend as many as possible.

After a great deal of hard work and negotiation, the visual display was finally completed on the Friday afternoon.

Paul sent an email informing his team that a visual management meeting would be held around the visual display each Monday at 11 a.m. He requested that it be updated by 10 a.m. each Monday. This gave him one hour to carry out a scheduled process confirmation. He also requested that his team join him at 4 p.m. that day to complete a joint review.

Shortly before 4 p.m. on the Friday afternoon, Paul arrived at the visual display. He was alone and took a long, hard look at the finished product. There were certainly more charts than there had been before, but they all adhered to a standard. Each chart was a standard colour scheme and a standard size, and displayed the current and historical KPI performance in elegant simplicity.

Paul stood back and tested the visual display for status at a glance. There were now red 'X's at the top of each department, except for safety, which was green. There were a large number of red 'X's and red flags visible. The visual display certainly passed the one second test, but was lacking in showing what the problems and actions were; the actions board was so far empty of actions.

That's only to be expected, thought Paul. *The meetings will drive the recording of actions.*

Lost in his thoughts, Paul was startled to realise that the rest of his team and their deputies had joined him.

'A penny for them,' said Sarah.

'Sorry?' said Paul.

'A penny for your thoughts,' she said. 'You were obviously deep in thought.'

'Yes, sorry,' said Paul. 'I was miles away.'

'There's a lot of red on the visual display now,' said Brian. 'We certainly have our work cut out to improve the situation.'

'That's what we pay you for,' said Paul. 'Did everyone read the email about the first meeting on Monday?'

He looked around and saw that everyone was nodding.

'The challenge for Monday,' he continued, 'is for us all to be clear as to what the problems are and what we're currently doing about them. Looking at the visual display, we're not currently sticking to the one, three, ten principle. Before 10 a.m. on Monday I want you all to update the visual display to show the main causes driving the red "X"s and red flags. All you need to do is write them onto the charts by hand. We'll discuss the actions at the meeting. I'd also like you to select one of your KPIs and to start to construct a Pareto chart. I'll leave it up to your intuition as to which KPI you choose. The important thing is that we make a start.'

Sarah stepped forward. 'The most pressing action I need to take is to get my visual management set up at the lower levels. I honestly believe that once we get our supervisors involved, then many of these KPIs will turn green.'

'That's a good point,' said Paul. 'We currently don't have a visible schedule for the development of a visual management system at lower levels.'

Peter put up his hand. 'I'll make the schedule and pin it up,' he said. 'I'll print it in black and white and then we can colour it red or green each week to show where we are on track and where we are behind.' (Refer to Figures 14 and 14a.)

'I won't have it done for Monday's meeting, but I can commit to Wednesday.'

'That's great, thank you, Peter,' said Paul, making a note in his notebook.

'Shouldn't we also have a visible schedule for the changeover to the new computer system and new suppliers?' said Helen.

'That's another good point,' said Paul, 'yes, we should.'

'I'll pull that together then,' said Helen. 'I'll liaise with Peter and make it to the same standard. I'll have it done by next Wednesday also.'

'Thank you, team,' said Paul. 'I finally believe we have made a breakthrough. I look forward to the first visual management meeting. Please come prepared. See you all on Monday morning.'

VISUAL MANAGEMENT FOR SCHEDULES

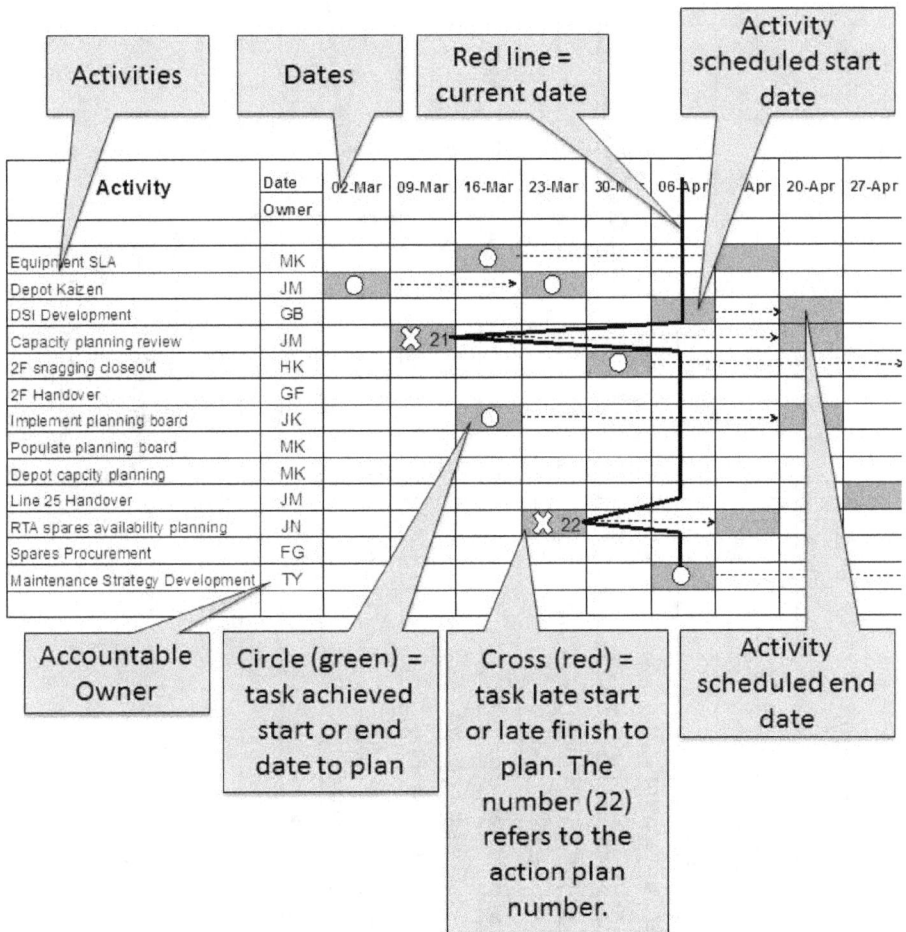

FIGURE 14

VISUAL MANAGEMENT FOR SCHEDULES – DETAIL 1

Activity	Date Owner	02-Mar	09-Mar	16-Mar	23-Mar	30-Mar	06-A
Equipment SLA	MK						
Depot Kaizen	JM	O					
DSI Development	GB						
Capacity planning review	JM		X 21				
2F snagging closeout	HK						
2F Handover	GF				O		
Implement planning board	JK						
Populate planning board	MK						
Depot capcity planning	MK						
Line 25 Handover	JM						
RTA spares availability planning	JN				X 22		
Spares Procurement	FG						
Maintenance Strategy Development	TY						O

X = Late start or finish
O= On time start or finish

Progress line showing progress as measured at the 6th April. A back spike = task behind schedule

FIGURE 14a

Chapter 8

Meeting mayhem

Paul looked around the room at his team – they were all talking at once. Peter and Helen, who'd brought their deputies along for the experience, were trying to draw them into the debate to reinforce their own positions, Sarah was practically shouting to make herself heard and Brian kept repeating, 'You don't understand!' like a stuck record.

'Silence!' shouted Paul, and they all stopped talking and turned to face him. 'Thank you,' he said. 'Now, let's try and sum up where we are. Be clear that I'm not starting any fresh discussions at this point, or reopening any we've had so far.' He looked at Peter's deputy. 'Simon, would you be so kind as to record the actions we've agreed on the flip chart?'

'Yes, of course,' said Simon, and he stood up, walked over to the board and uncapped a pen, ready to write.

They went around the table, each calling out their agreed actions. It didn't take long; by the time Simon had finished writing, the list was depressingly short.

In contrast to the frenetic discussion Paul had called a halt to some ten minutes earlier, the team were subdued. Few words were spoken, and those that were uttered came out in hushed, flat tones.

'Okay, people, that's it for today,' Paul said. It was clear he wasn't the only one who'd had enough.

As people gathered up their papers and filed out, each looked drained.

***

Back in his own office, Paul sat at his desk and reflected on the day so far. Three hours had been spent trying to review the visual display, three hours with Paul, his heads of department and two of their deputies – what on earth had that cost?

The purpose of the meeting had been to focus on the problems surfaced by the visual display. Paul had been expecting a short, focused meeting, with people concentrating on the facts and proposing solutions, but instead everyone had waffled on, then started defending their own situation and blaming their colleagues for the problems they faced. Paul was also frustrated by the use of vague language in the meeting. He lost count of the number of times he heard words like, 'I think', 'I believe', 'I'll try', 'hopefully' and 'possibly'. The meeting had dragged out into a colossal waste of time and then ended in a bun fight.

There was the knock on effect to take into account, as well … they would all now be playing catch up due to the time lost and, since very few actions had been defined, a further meeting was still required. It all conspired to make their targets even harder to hit.

Paul sighed; it seemed they hadn't made as much progress as he'd hoped, and that he wasn't as adept at implementing and using this new system as he'd believed. And he now had just one week left of the three Ed had given him to get visual management up and running.

He thought about his personal obligations and his heart sank. At the weekend he and Rebecca had toured the nursing homes she'd identified as being suitable for her mother, and of course the one they liked best was also the most expensive. Buoyed by the successes of the previous week, he'd assured her that wouldn't be a problem and encouraged her to go ahead and take the next steps in the process. He'd have to tell her about the situation he faced at work … that he might not have a job … that the nursing home and the house move were no longer an option. She'd be devastated.

Then he remembered the conversation he'd had with Mike Bailey, when he'd found out Mike and Mariam Khan had not only survived the takeover of their company, but prospered from it. 'And if they can, I can,' he muttered to himself. Reinvigorated, he picked up the phone and tapped in Mike's number.

After they'd exchanged pleasantries, Paul got to the point.

'Mike, I think I need to come and see how you run your review meetings. We've just had our first one and it was a shambles.'

Mike laughed. 'I can remember going through something similar myself when I was at about the stage you're at now. And your timing's great – I have my weekly meeting scheduled for tomorrow morning at ten thirty. You are certainly welcome to come along and join us.'

'Okay, thanks, Mike. See you tomorrow!'

Chapter 9

Mike's formula for effective VM review meetings

Paul woke early, and with a deep sense of anxiety. He felt motivated but at the same time worried; he had an urgent need to find the missing pieces of the puzzle. He eased out of bed, leaving his wife sleeping soundly, showered quickly, dressed, and silently left the house without even turning on the lights.

The roads were almost deserted and Paul made quick progress towards Mike's company. Alone with his thoughts – which were running wild – he suddenly realised that he was only a few miles away from his destination. Paul wanted nothing more than to meet up with Mike and start getting answers to his questions, and he hoped he was at work early. He called Mike's mobile phone; it rang through to his voice mail and Paul cursed in exasperation. Driving through a small town and seeing that all the shops were still closed, Paul suddenly realised that he was much too early. He cursed again; Mike was likely to still be at home in bed at this hour, or at best having breakfast.

I'm losing it, he thought to himself.

The shops disappeared and Paul pressed on, ready to accelerate onto the dark country roads. At the very edge of the town he spotted a small health club set back from the road, and the lights were on. He slowed the car and pulled into the car park.

The club was members only, but Paul convinced the lone attendant that he was interested in joining and was granted a free session to check out the facilities. He purchased some swimming shorts and was given a complimentary towel.

The swim was refreshing and Paul worked hard whilst his mind raced through everything that had happened over the last few days. He felt so close and yet still so far away from a solution that worked. Never before in his life had Paul felt such a deep need to make something work. To fail after all this effort was too painful to consider, and the prize of success was also exciting. He had pushed himself so far out of his comfort zone there was nothing left to fear other than failure.

After powering through a full forty lengths and nearly burning himself out, Paul relaxed in the steam room. He started to think about life in general, about his wife and how he had some making up to do when he got home. He watched the BBC news whilst he dressed, but he was more lost in his thoughts than listening to what was going on in the world.

Paul left the health club feeling as refreshed and relaxed as he could hope for. He drove slowly towards his destination. Minutes later, his mobile phone rang: Mike was calling.

'Hi,' said Mike, 'you're an early bird this morning, Paul; sorry I missed your call.'

'Sorry, Mike,' replied Paul. 'I was so eager to meet you today I totally forgot what time it was.'

'No problem.' Mike laughed. 'I assume you're on your way over to us, then?'

'Actually, I'm now just outside the gates and I'm hoping you can let me in.'

'I'll be waiting in the car park to meet you and then I suggest we get some coffee.'

***

Paul and Mike shook hands in the car park and made their way into the building. They walked over to a small kitchen area in an open-plan office, and Mike poured them each a cup of black coffee from a pot.

'No sugar or milk, I'm afraid,' he said, 'just black and pure. It'll wake you up, I promise you.' He smiled. 'So, Paul, why don't you tell me what has happened since we last met.'

They drank slowly as Paul brought Mike up to speed with everything that had happened. Mike listening intently, nursing his coffee; he smiled occasionally and nodded often.

As Paul was beginning to convey his frustrations, Mike cut in, 'So, in summary, the meeting took too long and lacked direction?'

'Yes. That's the short version, anyway.'

'Have you tried using the 5 Whys method of root cause analysis?' (Refer to Appendix 14.)

'No', said Paul. 'I've heard of it but never used it.'

'Let's try it now,' said Mike. 'All we have to do is keep asking "Why?"'

Paul shrugged. 'Okay, if you think it might help me.'

'So, Paul, why did your meeting take too long?'

'Because people wouldn't shut up, they weren't brief and they wandered off scope.'

'Why did they do that?'

'Because they didn't know when to shut up and stick to the purpose of the meeting.'

'Good,' said Mike. 'Why didn't they know when to shut up and stick to the purpose of the meeting?'

'Because … I suppose … they didn't know how to and … I didn't know when and how to tell them.'

'Why is that?'

'Well', said Paul, 'they … I mean, I … no, I mean *my team and I* didn't have any guidelines to follow.'

'Why not?'

'Because we haven't defined any guidelines or rules,' said Paul, the obvious realisation suddenly striking him. It was a real breakthrough moment.

'There you are, then,' said Mike, 'I think you now know what to do.'

'Do I really have to go to those lengths, though?' said Paul. 'I always feel that when I'm dealing with adults, people should know what they need to do. Surely everyone can see the problem like I do?'

'I used to think that, too,' said Mike, 'but I've learned over the years that everybody sees things differently and has different standards. I now believe that it is management's job to bring people together, and to agree common standards. It works, and believe me, in the long run they'll thank you for it.'

'Okay, I'm happy to learn from your experience,' said Paul.

'I'd also recommend you and your team learn to be clear and concise with written and verbal information. There's a book by Joseph McCormack, *Brief: Make a Bigger Impact by Saying Less,* that I think you would all benefit from reading.'

Paul made a note of the title and author.

Mike glanced at his watch. 'Time for me to go and do my process confirmation,' he said. 'You just take a moment; I'll come back and get you for the meeting.'

Paul nodded; he appreciated the space. He finished his coffee and placed both cups in the sink, then quickly recapped the notes he'd made in his notebook over the past couple of weeks. He'd learned so much!

Just as he finished, Mike reappeared, and led the way across the office to a small room at the back, where a number of people had already started to gather. Paul recognised the visual displays and 'Actions' boards. He quickly scanned them to understand where the problem areas were. As there were ten minutes to go before the start of the meeting, Mike introduced Paul to a number of people. Checking his watch again, he walked over to the left hand wall and grabbed a piece of paper that was Blu-Tacked to it, then pulled out a pen and began ticking off names. Paul could see that the paper was an attendance register and Mike was visibly checking off the names of the people in the room (refer to Figure 15).

VISUAL MANAGEMENT ATTENDANCE TRACKER

Team	Resource Attendance Chart Month - January													
	1	2	3	4	5	6	7	8	9	10	11	12	13	14
G Sale	O	O	O	O	O	O	O	O	O	O	O	O	O	
B Cole	O	O	O	O	O	O	O	O	O	O	O	O	X	
B Dunns	O	O	O	O	O	O	O	O	O	O	O	O	O	
M Robson	O	O	O	O	O	O	O	O	O	O	O	O	O	
R Doon	O	O	O	O	X	O	O	O	O	O	O	O	O	
D Jackson	O	O	O	O	O	O	O	O	X	O	O	O	O	
B Good	O	O	O	O	O	O	O	X	O	O	O	O	X	
J Stevens	O	O	O	O	O	O	O	O	O	O	O	O	O	
D Holister	O	O	O	O	O	O	O	O	O	O	O	O	O	

Date of meeting — 9

O (Green) - attendance

X (Red) – non-attendance

FIGURE 15

'Is that really necessary?' Paul asked. 'It's a bit like being at school, isn't it?'

Mike gave him a wry smile. 'It works, that's all I know. I didn't use to do it and I had a problem with attendance. I started doing this and the attendance problem went away.' He shrugged and passed the paper over so that Paul could see it fully. Listed on the page were Mike's department heads and their deputies and there were ticks against people's names for the last six weeks. Paul could see red crosses against two names prior to that, but there had been no repeat non-attendances until this week; Mike had put red crosses against three names, two deputies and one department head.

'Where are those people?' asked Paul. 'It's not quite time yet, how do you know they won't attend?'

'They're on holiday.'

'What happens if people are late? Do you still give them a red cross?'

'Yes,' replied Mike, 'and we lock them out – although I've only had to do it twice.'

Mike noticed the look of shock on Paul's face and laughed. 'It's all done with a light-hearted approach,' he said. 'If you keep it light-hearted then people get the message, but no one gets offended. If people repeatedly fail to adhere to standards, then I bring that up with them during their one-to-one monthly coaching meeting. I assume you have those with your own team?'

Paul nodded.

Mike walked over to the wall and stuck the attendance register back in its place. He then removed an A3 sheet of paper, headed 'Agenda' (refer to Figure 16).

'This agenda states our purpose for running the meeting,' said Mike, 'and also captures the outcomes we expect to achieve by the end of it. The running order and how much time is allowed for each section of the meeting is also described.' Mike passed the sheet to Paul.

'As you can see, Paul, the agenda is broken down into minutes and the whole meeting is designed to take a maximum of twenty-five minutes. This allows us to communicate how the meeting will run and how brief people are expected to be with their reporting.'

Paul could see that each person was only allowed three minutes to present their visual display. He whistled silently; *wow*, he thought to himself, *that's tight!* He was keen to see how they'd manage to get all the necessary information across in the time allowed.

VISUAL MANAGEMENT MEETING AGENDA

Visual management review agenda				
DATE:	Every Tues	**Location**		Meeting Room 2
TIME:	11am			
PURPOSE:				
1. To review current performance to KPI targets - to identify problems, causes, impact, actions and escalations. 2. To review current progress to project schedules - to identify where we are behind, causes, impact, actions and escalations.				
Expected Outcome:				
1. Everyone clear on status and problem areas 2. Problems are clear and actions to move forward are agreed, written down, time bound and individually accountable. 3. Actions requiring escalation are agreed and written down. 4. Everyone goes away knowing what they need to do to solve problems and implement solutions				
Agenda				
Item	Presentation/Review	Resp	Time	Requirements and Notes
1	Confirm attendees	MB	1	Visual Attendance register
2	Review actions from last time	MB	3	All HOD clear on action situation
3	KPI Performance Review	HOD	10	3 mins each head of department - red only, 1,3,10
4	Project Schedule Performance Review	HOD	10	3 mins each head of department - red only, 1,3,10
5	Check actions SMART and complete	MB	2	One owner per action, timebound, outcomes clear.
6	Wrap up and summarise Escalations	MB	2	
7	End	Total	28	Minutes
Issued By		Mike Bailey		
Date		21/1/15		
Required Attendance				
Mike Bailey - Director				
Karl Clevenger (deputy Charlie Harris – R&D				
Marie Olsen (deputy Steve Wall – technical project development				

FIGURE 16

'We also have rules for the meeting,' said Mike, pointing to three sheets of A3 paper on the wall (refer to Figures 17-19).

VISUAL MANAGEMENT RULES

- Phones on silent
- Be on time
- Stand up
- Only one voice
- Take discussions outside the meeting
- Come prepared – know the facts
- Stand at the front when invited by the chair person and use the Visual Management to present to leader
- Be brief – don't talk about green status
- Offer solutions as well as problems
- Stick to your time slot
- Take discussions outside the meeting
- Use specific language – avoid vague words (e.g. try, hopefully, possibly)

FIGURE 17

VISUAL MANAGEMENT RULES – UPDATING THE VISUAL DISPLAY

- Update your visual display before 11 a.m. on the day of the meeting
- Update risks, progress and problems – place on red flags
- Update all graphs – place red X where below target
- Place red X or green O on title – a red X must be placed where targets are missed on key target plan or on any graph or where a red flag is placed on a risk

FIGURE 18

VISUAL MANAGEMENT RULES – CHAIRING THE MEETING

- Follow the agenda
- Invite people to talk at their Visual Display
- Challenge timeliness – inform people when they are running out of time
- Challenge breakage of the rules – but keep it light
- Record actions on the Actions Boards
- Ensure Actions Boards are completed and up to date

VISUAL MANAGEMENT RULES – LEADER'S GUIDELINES

- Review the Visual Management before the meeting and be clear on which areas you want more info or to challenge
- Ask questions and challenge the data when people present
- Request actions to be set as you deem necessary
- Make priorities clear
- Challenge deviation from the rules
- Create a healthy tension during the meeting
- Initial each Visual Management each week

FIGURE 19

'They are posted there permanently and everyone that attends these meetings is coached in the rules and the agenda.

'The general rules are those set for everyone during the meeting's proceedings and cover simple things such as putting mobile phones on silent and standing rather than sitting.

'There are also rules for the updating of the visual display. I believe you already understand how individual accountability is allocated for updating and reporting against each visual display?'

Paul nodded.

'Each accountable person is responsible for updating the information accurately and by a set time each week.' Mike pointed to the last set of rules. 'Finally, there are reporting rules for the people who have accountability for reporting against the visual display. They are focused around lean communication. I request that accountable people arrive prepared and deliver a three minute summary of the problem areas, the risks, the actions taken and the actions required. This includes escalation of the problem, allowing help to be requested where blockages to the solution are felt.'

'Do people present on the green KPIs?'

'No, that wastes time. We are here to resolve problems in the minimum time and we avoid discussing what is going on in general.'

'How do you make sure that everyone understands and sticks to the rules?' asked Paul.

'As I mentioned earlier, each person that attends the visual review meeting is given some coaching on the rules. I also send everybody an email copy of the rules so they have them to hand if they need to check up on anything. During the meeting, if anyone deviates from the rules, I stop them and point out the deviation. This is all that is required.

'Everyone here agrees with the rules because they're designed to keep the meeting as short and focused as possible. Nobody wants to spend more time in meetings than they absolutely need to, but we forget ourselves sometimes and have to be reminded.'

Paul nodded; it all made sense. Meetings that ran on and on and didn't stick to the point had been a source of irritation for him for years.

'Right, people,' said Mike, raising his voice, 'let's get started.' Everyone in the room became quiet and turned their attention towards him. 'First of all I'll review the progress against actions.' Mike walked over to the 'Actions' board, situated on the right hand wall. The actions were recorded on A3 paper attached to an A3 clipboard. Mike unhooked the clipboard from the wall.

'The first action was set for Dave Moore,' said Mike. Paul knew from the list that Dave was the deputy in the purchasing department. 'Dave, the action was for you to write a letter to the MD of LDM Ltd requesting his personal assurance of the timely delivery of the information we've requested.'

'I've done that,' came the reply, 'and I've received his letter of assurance.'

Mike took a green highlighter pen from a holder on the wall and crossed through the action.

'The next action is for Jane,' said Mike. Jane Armour was head of purchasing. 'Jane, did you investigate the problem with the quality of the documentation for order number 4M32?'

'Yes, I did,' replied Jane. 'We've completed the investigation and carried out root cause analysis. The root cause is the lack of a clear standard for the completion of that document. We propose to define a new standard, test it, and then train everybody to use it.'

'Excellent, Jane,' said Mike. 'I'd like to briefly review your problem-solving and rationale. Please see me at the end of this meeting and I'll diarise a meeting for us to review together.' Mike struck the action through with the green marker. He then took a pencil and added a quick action to the clipboard. Paul moved closer and read, 'Review problem-solving with Jane for 4M32 problem and agree next steps, action owner, Mike, date for completion, today.'

'The next action is for Ron.' Ron Granger was Cheryl Young's deputy in safety.

'I've not had time to complete my action,' said a tall man at the back of the room. Mike added a red 'X' to the right of the action.

'This isn't urgent,' said Mike, 'I'm not overly concerned that it's outstanding. When will you complete the action, Ron?'

'I promise I'll have it completed before the next meeting,' said Ron. Mike made a note of the new date for completion on the clipboard.

Mike continued to work through all the actions until they had either been struck through in green, or a red X had been added, together with a new date.

'The next item on the agenda is the review of performance against targets for each accountable area,' said Mike. 'Jane, you are the head of purchasing, will you please give us your summary.' Everyone turned to face the visual display and Jane walked to stand in front of her section; she faced the audience. Before Jane started to speak, Mike stepped in and said, 'For Paul's benefit, I am going to summarise what Jane is going to do. She has three minutes to identify what problems have caused her KPIs and schedules to fail to hit target. She'll identify the potential impact of this failure and identify what actions her team plan to take or have already taken to fix the problems. She'll identify any support she needs from me or other departments. Jane may request actions to be agreed and recorded. I'll listen to what she has to say and ask clarifying questions. I may request actions to be recorded.'

Mike offered the A3 action clipboard to Ron. 'Ron, would you please capture the actions going forward, for the remainder of this review meeting?'

Ron smiled, nodded and took the clipboard from Mike.

Mike continued. 'The test for Jane is for her to show that she has a good management grasp of her department's performance and problems. She demonstrates this by showing her ability to clearly and simply summarise in three minutes or less. Clarity and simplicity are a test of clear thinking. If you cannot clearly and simply summarise the situation, then you do not understand the situation yourself.

'Please go ahead, Jane.'

Jane began by explaining that her department was red status and that this was caused by a failure to achieve the target in one area and having a red flag status in another. The area of failure was a KPI for contract completion. The target was set at ten contracts per week, but only eight had been completed and fully signed off in the last week. Jane explained the impact of this was minor and that she had taken steps to enlist and rapidly train members of staff from another area to help clear the backlog. The problem had been caused by staff shortage due to illness in the contracts department, but this was a one off and not a repeating problem. Mike nodded and said he was happy with this, and asked her to move on.

Jane continued. 'I've also raised a red flag risk against our ability to meet the target date for the procurement of materials for the new dedicated computer server building project. I've raised this flag because we've not received the outline specification. I emailed Jim in the project department several times and also called to discuss the issue with him. I'm struggling to get him to understand that I only need some basic information about materials and not the whole specification.'

Karl Clevenger, head of R&D, stepped forward. 'I have a meeting with Jim tomorrow morning,' he said. 'I've had a similar problem before and I know that he can be pedantic sometimes. I have a good relationship with him now and I feel confident that I could help out here. I'm happy to take an action to help sort this out.'

'That's great,' said Mike. 'Ron, please record the action for Karl. However, if you are unable to resolve this issue at the meeting tomorrow morning, Karl, then I want you to report back to me before the end of the day.'

Karl nodded as Ron continued to write on the 'Actions' board. 'Okay, Mike, I'll do that.'

'Thank you,' said Jane. 'We're on target in all other areas. Do you have any other questions, Mike?' Mike shook his head and Jane walked to the side of the room.

Mike turned to his left and addressed the young man standing next to him. 'Karl, you are up next.'

Karl walked to stand in front of his visual display.

'We are all green,' said Karl pointing to the green 'O' at the top of his visual display. 'I'd like to mention the work we have been completing on the China project and say a thank you to Ron for the support his team has been giving us to …'

Mike stepped in and raised his hand. 'Thank you, Karl, I have to stop you,' he said pointing to the rules – *be brief and don't talk about the green.*

'Oh, yes; sorry,' said Karl.

Mike looked around the room and said, 'Cheryl, you are up next.'

Cheryl Young, head of safety, walked to the front of the room and announced that her department was red due to one target being missed.

'The red "X" is because we have failed to complete our audits to plan,' she explained. 'We've now missed this target for the last four weeks and the quick fix solutions we've implemented are not working to get us back on track and keep us there.'

'What's the impact?' asked Mike.

'The implications are serious,' she said. 'We have a legal obligation to undertake these audits in a timely manner, and in the worst situation it could mean we fail to spot a problem that leads to environmental harm.'

'Do you understand the root cause of failure to hit the target?' asked Mike.

Cheryl shook her head. 'My team have started to collect information on the problem, and have promised me a Pareto chart by the end of the day. Once I receive that I'll start an analysis of the problem.'

Mike nodded and said, 'This is now becoming an urgent matter. I'd like you and your team to take the largest issue on the Pareto chart and complete a 5 Whys analysis using an A3 problem-solving pro forma to show your analysis of the problem.' (Refer to Figure 20.)

'I want to see what you identify as the root cause.' Mike turned to Ron. 'Ron, I'd like an action to be recorded for Cheryl to complete the first draft of this problem-solving pro forma by lunchtime tomorrow. Cheryl, I would like you to present your analysis and recommendation to fix the root cause to me in my office at 1 p.m. tomorrow.' Ron and Cheryl both nodded.

'I also want you to set up daily visual management with your team for this issue,' said Mike. 'This requires short interval control and that means you review adherence to the audit plan at least every day with your team, record problems, and decide daily actions to improve. A ten minute daily team meeting will be required for this and it will help you collect the information for your Pareto chart.'

'I've captured that,' said Ron.

Cheryl nodded. 'No problem,' she said.

A lady that Paul had not noticed before suddenly spoke up. 'Cheryl, I may be able to help you. I have a lot of experience with those types of audits from a previous role. If you'd like my input, please see me after the meeting.'

'Thank you, Marie,' said Cheryl. 'Can I ask, what experience have you had?'

Mike stepped forward. 'Please take this conversation outside of the meeting. Thank you, Marie, for volunteering to help, but we need to move on. And since Steve is on holiday, you're up next for technical project development.'

'Okay, thanks, Mike.' Marie stepped forward and cleared her throat.

'This is Marie's first time reporting on the visual display,' Mike whispered to Paul.

'We have one area of target failure,' Marie said, 'against a milestone on the schedule tracking the design and development of a new computer system for a large client. The design concept drawing was due last week, but has not been received. We've been let down by the design department and the consequences could be failure to deliver to the customer as promised. We need to escalate the issue to you, now, Mike.'

Bruce Davidson, the manager of the design department, was in attendance at the meeting and he interrupted and started to explain his problems for failing to deliver. He was rather emotional and defensive. Other people in the meeting started to chip in with their own comments and opinions and the room very quickly started to buzz with conversation.

Mike raised his hand. 'There is a conversation growing here,' he said, pointing to the rules – *take conversations outside the meeting*. 'Please take the conversation outside of this meeting. This issue concerns me and I need for us to stay on target with this customer. Ron, please record an action for me to organise a meeting with Marie and Bruce to discuss and resolve this issue.' Ron nodded and scribbled away. 'Thank you, Ron. As this is urgent, please record that this meeting needs to be set up before the end of the day.'

The review continued until all accountable people had given their summary of the visual status. Several more actions were set. Mike asked Ron to read through all actions defined and checked to ensure each one had one accountable owner and a due date for completion. Mike then summarised his understanding of the priority issues and made it clear that his door was always open to discuss and support these matters. He thanked everyone for attending and then closed the meeting. Paul checked his watch; everything had been completed in twenty-five minutes.

As people began to disperse, Paul gave Mike his sincere thanks and said he would not take up any more of his time.

A3 PROBLEM SOLVING REPORT

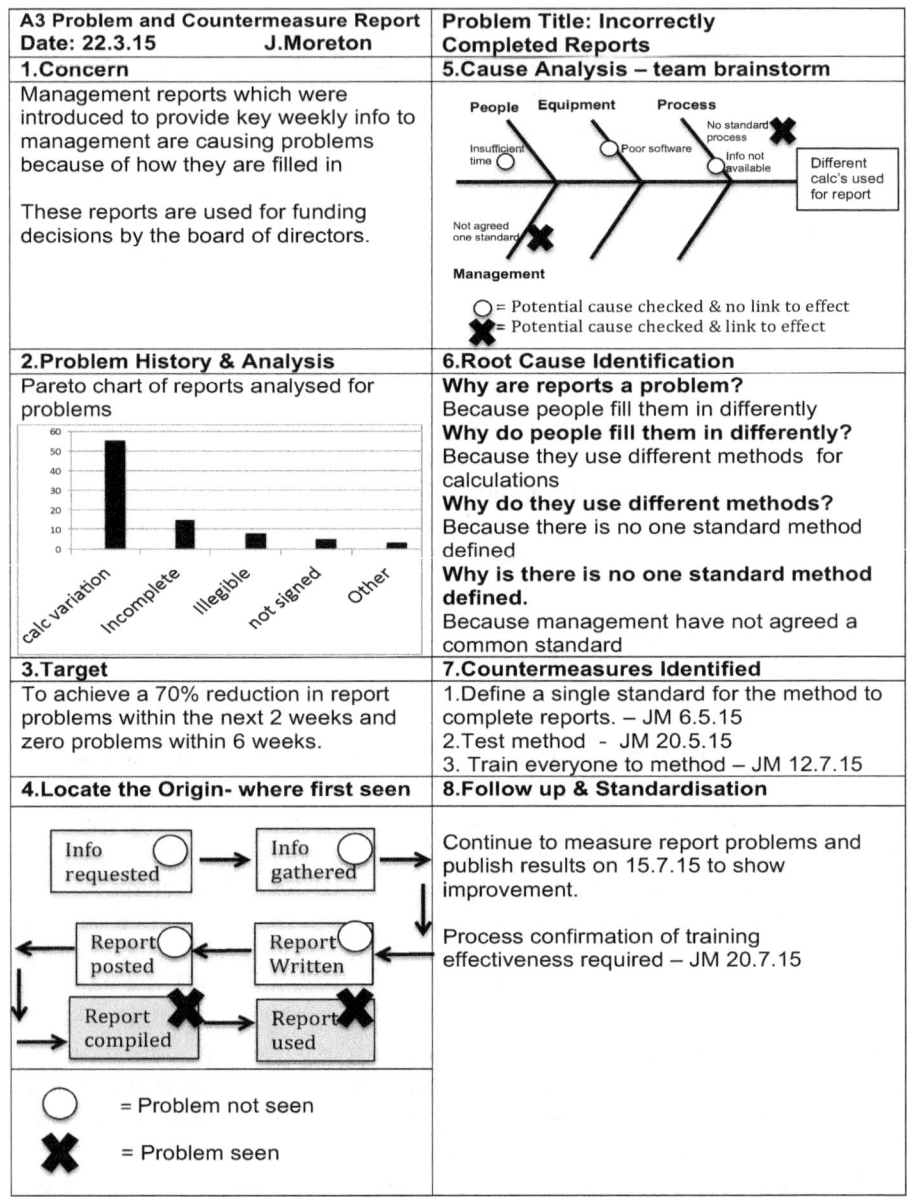

FIGURE 20

'Glad I could be of assistance,' said Mike. 'Believe me, I've been stuck myself, so I know what it's like. I honestly now think you have a good chance of making visual management work, Paul. You know enough about the techniques, behaviours and mindset. You just need to put them all together and lead by example.'

Yes, thought Paul, *I can now see how this all fits together, I'm finally starting to believe, and I know what I need to do.*

Filled with renewed determination, Paul drove back to his office.

JON MORETON

Chapter 10

Solid progress – and a further challenge

Next morning, Paul pulled into the car park and reversed into a parking space. Every time he did that now he was reminded of that morning when everything changed; that first painful meeting with Ed and the eventful episodes that had followed. He burst through the doors to the reception area and called a greeting to Nigel Harrison, the receptionist.

Walking down the corridor towards his office, Paul noticed that he had a queue of people waiting for him.

'Good morning all,' he said. 'Please come in. How can I help?' He was determined not to get sidetracked this morning and intended to keep his interactions with these people as brief as possible.

First through the door was Ann Oliver, Sarah's deputy. She followed Paul in as soon as he opened the door.

'I need a car to send the supervisors on a visit to see Mike Bailey and Mariam Khan,' she said. 'All the pool cars are out; can they borrow yours?'

'Yes,' said Paul without even thinking it through. He handed her his car keys. 'But before you go, how are the visual displays for the supervisors coming along?'

'Really well,' said Ann. 'We have all the materials on order. We've opted for mobile visual display boards so they can be wheeled in and out of the meeting areas, but stored in the most visual positions on the shop floor. The boards are due for delivery tomorrow, and Stuart and Graham have promised to have them all set up by the end of the day. We're on track to have them fully populated by the end of the week.'

'Fantastic,' said Paul. He gave the thumbs up to Ann and she left.

As Paul started to walk towards his desk, he noticed the chart on the wall tracking the time he spent out of the office: he was barely meeting the target set by Ed. Instead of sitting down and receiving people in his office as he normally would, he decided that he would do something different.

'If you want to talk to me, you need to walk with me,' he said to the remaining people. 'I'm going to see what is going on in the real world.'

The flock of people followed him out. As they walked, Paul signed off several purchase requisitions and listened patiently as people spelled out their concerns. Apparently Ed had been walking around over the last couple of days, asking lots of questions; there were rumours that operations was going to be moved to another location; absenteeism was very high; the heating system was playing up again.

After walking through two departments, talking briefly with the supervisors, and feeling satisfied that everything appeared to be running smoothly, Paul came upon a group of people standing around looking lost.

'What's the problem?' he asked.

'We can't enter the control room, Mr Wayman,' said a young woman.

'Why not?' asked Paul. 'What's stopping you going in?'

'The personal protective equipment cupboard is empty,' she said. 'We can't go in without the correct PPE.' She pointed to a sign on the door that prohibited entry without the correct equipment.

'Who is sorting this out for you?'

'Colin has gone to find a supervisor,' she said. 'Hopefully he won't be too long.'

Paul waited with the group and after ten minutes the supervisor arrived with a box full of PPE. He proceeded to hand out the equipment and the team of people shuffled through the door into the control room. Paul watched as he then placed the remainder of the PPE in the cupboard. The supervisor noticed that Paul was watching and smiled sheepishly.

Paul walked over to him. 'Hi,' said Paul, 'it's Tony, isn't it?'

'Yes,' said Tony. 'Sorry, Mr Wayman, this must look bad.'

'Well, I'm concerned that we just lost half an hour of productive time.'

'I'm sorry. I've sorted it out now and I'll make sure it doesn't happen again.'

At that moment Sarah arrived. 'What's up?' she asked.

Paul explained what had happened and Sarah gave the supervisor a hard look.

'I'm not blaming anybody,' said Paul. 'I just want to understand how we can stop it happening again.'

Tony put his head down and remained quiet.

'Let's see if we can work through this together,' said Paul.

Sarah nodded.

'Why did the cupboard run out of PPE?' asked Paul. He looked at Tony quizzically.

'To be honest, I forgot to fill it up,' he said. 'I'm sorry I—'

Paul cut him off and asked softly, 'Why did you forget, Tony?'

'Because I'm really busy at the moment trying to sort a lot of other things out. I didn't realise it was empty until I saw people standing around this morning.'

'That's fine,' said Paul, reassuring him. 'So if I understand you correctly, the department relies on you to either remember to keep the PPE cupboard topped up or to notice that it needs topping up?'

Tony nodded. 'Yes that's correct,' he said.

'Why is that?' said Paul.

'Because that's my responsibility and the way we do things,' said Tony. Paul could tell from his voice that he was starting to feel defensive.

'Okay,' he said. 'Could you identify a better system so that you don't need to remember, or could you make it easier to see that it needs topping up?'

'We could make it somebody else's responsibility,' said Tony. 'Someone that's not as busy as me, maybe.'

'That's not an option,' said Sarah. 'Everyone is very busy and the problem would just pass over to someone else.'

Tony looked nervous. 'Okay,' he said. 'Well, I'll need to think about it, but I'm fairly sure I could come up with something.'

'I'm setting you a challenge,' said Paul. 'Your challenge is to figure out a simple system to help you keep the cupboard topped up with PPE, a system that will ensure we don't lose any more time due to this problem.'

'When will I need to let you know?'

'I'll be here at the same time tomorrow. I'll come and find you and we can have a chat then.'

'Okay,' said Tony, 'I'll give you my ideas tomorrow, then.'

'Thank you, Tony, I look forward to hearing them. Have a good day and see you tomorrow.'

Paul and Sarah walked away together. 'That was interesting,' she said. 'If I had spotted that problem I would have given Tony a piece of my mind and told him to make sure he was better prepared in future. You didn't do that, Paul; instead, you asked him questions and then set him a challenge.'

'It's a simple technique called 5 Whys analysis,' said Paul. 'It helps to get to the root cause of the problem and avoid firefighting. I believe we can use it to challenge people to solve their own problems, especially when mistakes have been made. I want us all to start using 5 Whys. We need to start getting everybody used to solving problems, and solving them in a way that stops them coming back again.'

'Okay,' said Sarah. 'That makes sense. I'll give a try.'

As they walked, Sarah pointed out the areas where the daily visual management would be located. She also pointed out the processes where short interval control would be used.

Eventually they reached the area where their weekly visual display was located to find Peter and Brian, deep in conversation.

Paul turned to Sarah. 'Could you call Helen and ask her to join us?' he asked. 'I'd like to have a chat with all the heads of department.'

As Sarah moved away to call Helen on her mobile phone, Paul walked over to Brian and Peter.

'Don't go away, gentlemen,' he said. 'I want to talk to you all. Sarah's just calling Helen. As soon as we're all together we can make a start.'

A few minutes later, Helen walked briskly over to join them.

'Right,' said Paul. 'I think we all agree that our first attempt at a visual management meeting did not go well.'

Everyone nodded.

Paul explained the problem using the 5 Whys method and shared the conclusions he had drawn whilst talking to Mike. He also explained what he had seen at Mike's meeting, what it felt like and how it was a different approach.

'So we need to set some rules and guidelines,' said Helen, 'and be very clear on our purpose, agenda and outcomes.'

'I believe that is exactly what we need,' said Paul. 'We also need to get used to being leaner with our communication. The people at Mike's meeting focused only on the problem areas, their reports were very brief and very factual.'

'Shall we start to brainstorm what our rules need to be?' asked Peter.

'No,' said Paul, 'we don't have time for that. I want to start using the rules that Mike has already developed and then refine them to suit us as we go.'

'That makes sense to me,' said Sarah. 'When will we get to see them?'

'I've emailed them to our two students. They're going to format them, print them out in big lettering and stick them up here in the visual display area this morning. They'll also email a copy out to each of you and your deputies, together with a copy of an agenda.'

Sarah nodded.

'I want to meet each of you here today, with your deputies, for a coaching session. Please book yourselves a half hour slot in my diary for this afternoon. I'll explain the rules, the attendance register, the purpose, the agenda and outcomes. The challenge for each of you and your deputies will be to demonstrate to me that you can summarise your visual display in three minutes or less.'

'Three minutes!' said Brian. 'That's going to be really tough.'

'In that case I expect you to prepare for it,' said Paul, 'because I'm going to be timing each of you. Your challenge is to take me through one, three, ten on your visual display, and I also want to know what other actions we need to take to support you, all within the three minutes. You cannot afford to waffle, over-explain or digress. You need to focus on the reds and get to the point quickly, using facts and with no finger-pointing. We'll also run all meetings as standing meetings from now on; this will help us focus on keeping them short.'

Everyone nodded, although Paul noticed they looked a little shell-shocked. Peter and Brian turned to leave.

'Wait a minute,' said Paul. 'Before you go, I want a quick review of our plans to set up daily visual management. I took a walk around the company this morning and it didn't take long for me to spot a problem. As you are all aware, Ed has also been walking around and if I can spot problems then so can he.' He looked at each of his department heads in turn. 'We need to start making problems more visible, get people talking about them and solving them on a daily basis. I want the visual displays set up this week so that we can start running them next week. The week after next I want us all to start coaching people on the 5 Whys method of solving problems and to start fixing problems at the systems level. I also want all managers to start process confirmation on a daily basis and to use flag and follow up. That means we'll all be reviewing visual displays every day and following up with people on their commitments to solve problems and take action every day. I would also like process confirmation to be extended to checking on all standards. At the start this will be a tough challenge, but we'll save time by stopping the repeat problems that cost us time as well as results. We'll also save time by becoming leaner in our communication methods.'

'Okay,' said Brian.

'I've just signed off one group of supervisors to go and take the tour of Mike and Mariam's company,' said Paul. 'How soon can the next group be sent on the visit?'

'Tomorrow,' said Sarah, and Helen, Brian and Peter nodded their agreement.

'Good,' said Paul. 'When will the workshops be run with the supervisors to work with them on the KPI trees?'

'Thursday,' said Helen. 'Four sessions have been planned, two in the morning, two in the afternoon.'

'Excellent,' said Paul. He walked over to the schedules pinned on the wall. The action bars were currently all green, showing they were on target.

'These schedules are showing we are currently on track to get all the visual displays set up this week,' he said, 'and we can't afford to slip. I want a ten minute daily meeting to review progress against these plans, starting at 13.00 today. This will be a ten minute meeting, so each of you needs to give me a summary in one minute or less. I'm only interested in the red "X"s and the red flags on the schedules. Any more questions?'

Brian, Helen, Sarah and Peter remained silent.

'Good,' said Paul. 'I'll see you all at the 13.00 review, and then at your half hour coaching session.'

***

Prior to the 13.00 meeting, Paul continued to walk around the workplace. He talked to people about how the company systems worked, what their problems were and what actions were currently being taken to fix them. In each area he asked everyone to stop work for ten minutes whilst he gave a short talk on the changes taking place.

'Our new owners expect better results,' he explained. 'If we deliver better results we are all safe. We don't want to all work harder, so we need to find a way to work smarter. If we can start to solve the small problems we all experience, daily, weekly and monthly, then we'll improve our results. We want to remove the frustrations, the hassles, the delays, and make work easier to do. We're going to set up visual management to help us do this. It will show us what our targets are, how we are doing and what problems we need to solve. We'll then work together to fix the problems. The new challenge is that we all need to become good problem-solvers – the more brains the better.'

***

Paul ran a strict agenda at the 13.00 meetings. He took Mike's advice and kept the process light. He was ruthless at challenging the rules, but achieved it with a light and humorous touch. It was a great success.

To start with, Brian and Peter really struggled with the one minute summary. Paul repeatedly stopped them when they digressed or started talking generally about what they had been doing rather than focusing on the problem areas.

By Thursday, everyone was getting the hang of it and Paul started to notice some friendly competition creeping in.

By Friday the meeting was starting on time at 13.00 and was finished within the allotted ten minute time slot.

***

On Thursday morning, Paul stopped off to see Tony and hear what his proposed solution was to the challenge he had been set. It was simple; he set up a simple visual check sheet in his office for all the things he needed to check on a daily basis. He also put a notice inside the cupboard saying, 'If there are only four sets of equipment left after you take yours from the cupboard, ring Tony on Ext. 321 and let him know.'

Paul was delighted and made sure Tony knew he'd done well.

On Thursday afternoon, Paul went along to one of the supervisor workshops. Helen and Sarah were running it and they had managed to fully engage the supervisors in a lively debate. As Paul walked in he saw that one of the supervisors, Ella Rhodes, was explaining an idea she had for improving the visual displays.

'As I understand it,' she said, "we'll need to lead the daily meetings with our team members. At our level, it doesn't make sense to ask the team members to present against areas of accountability because they don't have them in the same way that supervisors and managers do.'

Other supervisors were nodding their agreement with Ella.

'Therefore,' continued Ella, 'we will only have one set of KPIs per supervisor and we'll talk through the results, but ask team members to define the problems and contribute ideas for solutions. I have noticed that all the KPIs fit neatly under five headings: safety, quality, cost, delivery and people. Each set of KPIs could be headed by a letter, S, Q, C, D and P. Each letter could be divided into thirty-one sections to represent the days of the month.'

She drew her idea onto the white board.

'Each day, we'll review all the KPIs under each letter with our teams. For example, we would start with safety and review all safety KPIs, then we would move to quality and review the quality KPIs, then the delivery KPIs, then cost, and finally the people KPIs. If the safety KPIs are all green, then we colour in a strip of the S in green. If any are red, we colour a strip in red and ask for problems and actions. This will show at a glance how we are performing against our KPIs over the whole month and highlight areas where we have the biggest issues. I think this would be a better scoreboard because it will show us how we are doing across the month and not just day-to-day. We could also target two minutes for each letter and this would ensure the meeting is completed within ten minutes.'

Paul put his hand up.

'That's a great idea, Ella,' he said. 'What sort of KPIs would go under the P for people?'

'We could put our training KPIs under P,' she said, 'and also absenteeism. Skill matrices and skills targets could fit in this section, too.'

'Fantastic,' said Paul. 'I love the way it ensures that we always start by talking about safety as the first item on the agenda. Could you make up an example visual display, please? We'll try it, and show it to the others.'

A visual display using SQCDP was quickly put together and shown to all other supervisors (refer to Figures 21 and 21a).

The idea met with nearly unanimous approval and was adopted as the new standard. Paul personally thanked Ella and made sure everyone knew that this was her idea.

***

The plans to set up daily visual management remained on target and all managers ensured that their areas were ready for the following Monday.

On that Monday morning, Paul came into work full of excitement. He avoided his office and headed directly to see the visual displays in their various locations. He carried out a process confirmation on every one and signed them all. Overall, he was impressed with their adherence to a common standard. He spoke directly to each supervisor about the importance of giving visual management a fair chance to show what it could deliver. He asked them to convey this message to their teams.

The first meetings started to be held on a daily basis around the visual management boards and recorded actions started to appear. Ed's signature also started to appear on the visual displays.

The weekly 11 a.m. visual management meeting was much tighter than before – the short daily meetings had helped Paul's team learn the art of lean communication. Although many of the KPIs were red, the actions to address them were clear and concise. Where there was a lack of clarity on a problem, the conversation was cut short and an action was set for someone to go away and collect the facts. Paul maintained a tight grip on the meeting and created an air of positive tension.

SQCDP VISUAL DISPLAY

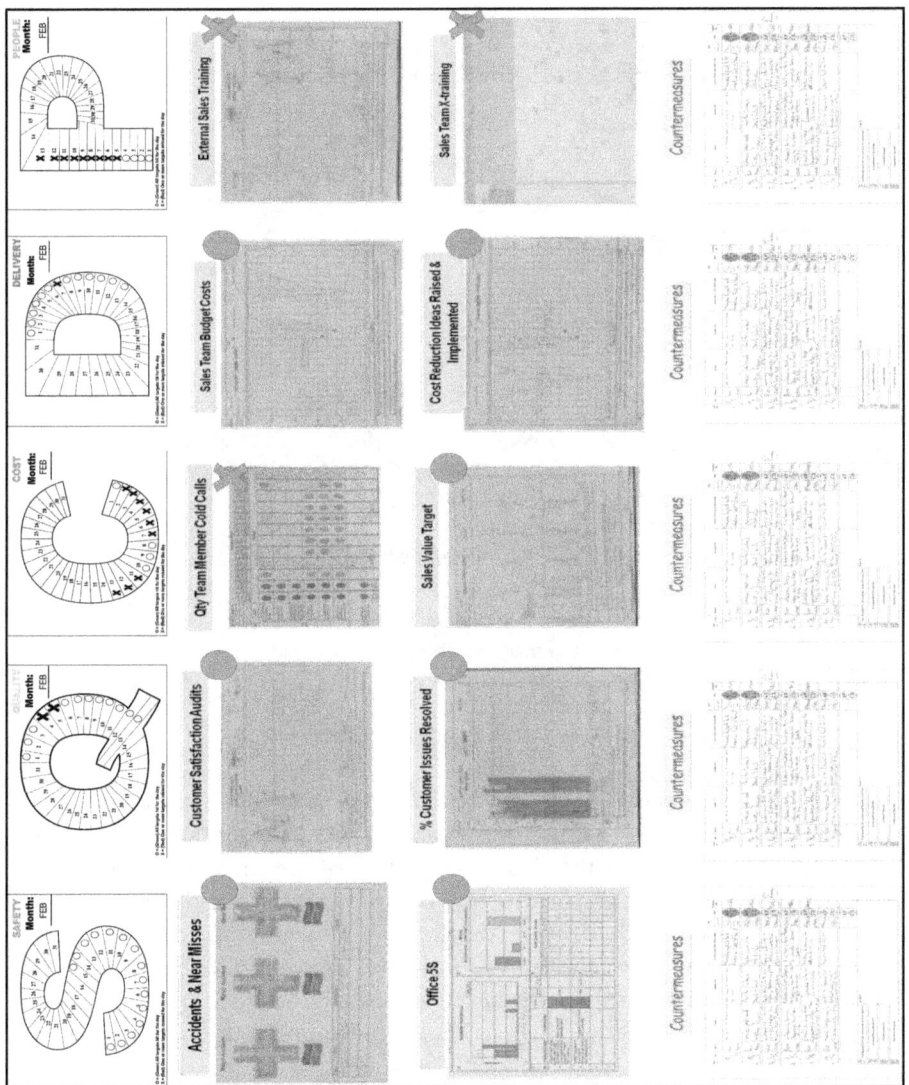

FIGURE 21

SQCDP VISUAL DISPLAY DETAIL

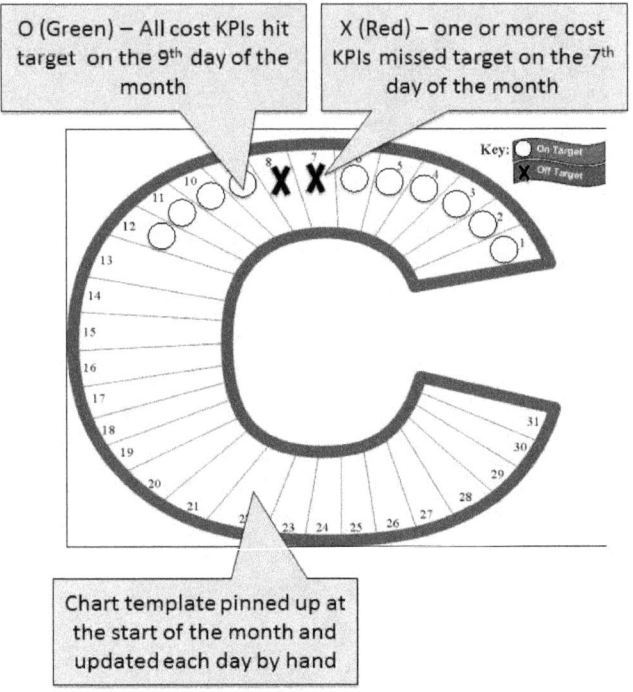

FIGURE 21a

He divided the meeting into two halves. The first half was dedicated to reviewing KPIs on the KPI visual display. Each accountable person was allowed three minutes for this. The second half of the meeting was dedicated to reviewing the schedules for the new computer system and for the change of suppliers. The schedules were displayed on separate visual displays and divided by accountability similar to the KPIs. Two minutes per person was allowed for the reviews of the visual schedules.

At the end of the meeting, just as Paul was wrapping up and pointing out the priorities for the week, Ed suddenly appeared.

Paul stopped talking and everyone was quiet in anticipation of what he might say.

'I want to congratulate you all,' said Ed. 'You have achieved a significant milestone in your application of visual management. I can clearly see how all the daily visual management boards feed up to your weekly summary. You have now achieved status at a glance and the application of one, three, ten. Your next challenge is to show that you can use it to deliver better results.' Ed then turned and walked away.

As Paul was walking back to his office he had a wonderful feeling of success. Ed had congratulated the team and that surely meant he had now successfully achieved the challenge that Ed had set three weeks ago.

It was close, Paul thought to himself, *but I did it.* He felt good about himself for the first time in what seemed like a long time.

When Paul finally returned to his office, he sat down and opened his laptop for the first time that day. He felt tired and relieved, but as soon as he opened his email folder a message from Ed caught his eye.

Well done, Paul. You have achieved your challenge of setting up visual management. Your next challenge is to demonstrate results. You have six weeks. Please do not disappoint me.

JON MORETON

Chapter 11

Getting results with visual management

Throughout the rest of the week, Paul attended each of the visual management daily meetings to show his support and to review the standard being achieved. After each meeting he carried out a short coaching session with his head of department to evaluate the standard of the meeting. Paul challenged, coached and supported his department heads to improve the running of the meeting to the defined standards. He asked them to coach their supervisors in the same way and he followed up to see how they ran their own coaching sessions with their supervisors.

At the start the supervisors were rather timid and many team members were sceptical and disinterested. As time went on, and with the visible support of Paul and his heads of department, the supervisors started to gain in confidence. People started to get the message – this was being driven from the top, it was serious, and wasn't going to go away as many fads and initiatives had in the past.

Problems started to be brought to the surface and after a few were successfully solved, the scepticism began to thaw. The personal benefits started to be felt: frustrations were removed; defective equipment was fixed and replaced; cost-effective upgrades were carried out; simple changes were made to make people's jobs easier; wasted time was reduced; new standards were defined for the quickest and easiest ways to do things.

The supervisors found to their surprise that many ideas for solutions were starting to come from team members. They recorded all ideas, implemented many of them and provided feedback to people individually on all of them. Problems that used to go to the weekly management meetings were now being solved at lower levels. The low tech, high touch systems also enabled everybody to get involved with the updating of the visual displays.

Helen started to feel a strong pull on her department's services. She found that she enjoyed the challenge. She coached her team to raise their game and the engineering team loved the fact that they could visibly see the impact of the improvements they helped to put in place.

During the next week, 5 Whys analysis began to be implemented. It was introduced gradually – each supervisor was challenged to pick one problem area per week and use 5 Whys analysis to get to the root cause of the problem. Paul led by example and demonstrated 5 Whys analysis on one problem at each of the supervisor daily meetings during the week. He then asked his heads of department to do the same for the following week. He also asked them to challenge and support their supervisors to start to do it in subsequent weeks. The focus for 5 Whys analysis was on whichever area, SQCD or P, showed the most red for the week.

Short interval control was also introduced and started to have a positive impact before the week was even over.

By the third week, the mood in the company had begun to feel more positive. People were becoming accustomed to visual management. Sarah noticed that an element of competition had started between the supervisors, and each supervisor was starting to pay attention to the visual displays of their peers.

A noticeable upward trend started to appear on many of the results KPIs. The productivity KPI was the most improved of all. The top level visual display showed green status for productivity and even though the target was due to be stepped up soon, in line with a scheduled improvement event, the performance was already above the new level: the highest ever achieved by the company.

Paul was very relieved to see these results and took a walk to see Sarah. He got there as she was conducting her daily review with her supervisors. As they concluded the review of actions, Paul walked over.

'I want to congratulate you all and say thanks for a fantastic result,' he said. 'Our productivity is now the best I have ever seen it and that's down to you and your efforts. Thank you and well done.'

Sarah and the team leaders smiled and said thank you in return.

'Actually, Paul,' said Sarah, 'I need to talk to you.'

'Of course,' said Paul. 'Shall we walk and talk? I'd like to walk over to the three areas where you've set up short interval control and review how it's working.'

'Okay,' said Sarah.

They started walking together and Paul asked, 'What did you want to talk to me about?'

'I have a problem,' she said. 'Don't worry, I also have an idea how to fix it.'

'Go on,' said Paul, 'I'm listening.'

'Well,' said Sarah, 'the improvements in productivity have surprised me. I've not even run one improvement workshop and we're already halfway towards our target.'

'That's not a problem,' said Paul, 'that's a fantastic result.'

'Yes,' said Sarah. 'The results are good and I've been thinking about why that is the case. In the past, I used to run one meeting per week with my supervisors. I estimate that we used to discuss and agree on actions for about ten problems at that meeting. Even then, we didn't use 5 Whys, so the actions tended to be just containments. Now that we are running our visual management systems, we agree actions on about five problems each day in both daily visual management and short interval control meetings. We also solve, on average, one escalated problem each day at the supervisor daily meeting. All in all this adds up to over two hundred problems being identified and actioned each week. That's a twenty-fold increase in the level of problem-solving compared to what we used to do.'

'Wow,' said Paul.

'On top of that,' said Sarah. 'I've noticed that most people are a little more enthusiastic about their jobs than they used to be. Even people doing very simple, repetitive tasks seem more upbeat and are trying that bit harder. Absenteeism has reduced and is now at its lowest level for years. What I'm getting at is that there appears to have been a productivity improvement just as a result of us paying more attention to people.'

'That's interesting,' said Paul.

'Yes, I thought so, too, so I looked it up on Google. It turns out it's a well-documented reaction called the Hawthorne effect. Quite simply, it's a positive effect brought about by paying people more attention. I think visual management, process confirmation and us managers getting out of our offices has all contributed towards the Hawthorne effect.' (Refer to Appendix 15.)

'This is all great news,' said Paul. 'So, what's the problem?'

'The problem,' said Sarah, 'is that I'm often pulled away from the front line and so are my supervisors, to the extent that I'm starting to worry that we'll not be able to sustain the level of performance we've achieved. We are now flat out supporting the front line and just about managing to keep on top of the actions to solve problems. We are constantly juggling to maintain a high level of front line support.'

'Why do you get pulled away?' asked Paul.

'Because of meetings,' said Sarah. 'Meetings are being booked in our online diaries and we can't keep refusing them. I've tried blocking out my time, but I then find that I just ending up missing out because I'm the only one that can't attend. The meeting doesn't get rearranged, it just goes ahead without me being there.'

'What sort of meetings are they?'

'All sorts, including customer meetings, safety meetings and HR reviews, and a lot of them are important ones that I really need to attend. The same problem applies to my supervisors. This disrupts our time on the shop floor and reduces our ability to offer support.'

'I see,' said Paul. 'You mentioned that you have a proposed solution. I hope you're not going to ask to employ another manager?'

'No,' said Sarah, 'I know that's not a viable solution. My idea is to create a standardised diary for everyone.' (Refer to Figure 22 and Appendix 16.)

STANDARD DIARY

	Mon	Tues	Wed	Thurs	Fri
8Am	Team Daily Visual Management Meetings				
9	Shop floor	Shop floor	Shop floor	Shop floor	Shop floor
10	Open Diary		Open Diary	Open Diary	Open Diary
11		Vis Man - management Team			
12		Open Diary			
1PM	Open for Meetings				Visual Project Review
2	Supervisor Daily Visual Management Meetings				
3	Open Diary	Open Diary	Open Diary	Open Diary	Open Diary
4					
5					

FIGURE 22

'I'm not with you,' said Paul, 'what does that mean?'

'It means,' said Sarah, 'we divide up the day into blocks of time. They could be half hour blocks, for example. We work out and agree when visual management, process confirmation and other activities need our time and we block these times out of the company diary. This will then stop other meetings and activities interfering with our work to support front line operations and ensure that important meetings are arranged during times I'm able to attend. For example, we could block out 9-11 a.m. and 2-3 p.m. for visual management, process confirmation and shop floor time, meaning other meetings are scheduled around that.'

Paul considered this idea. 'I like it,' he said. 'What can be more important than making sure we achieve the strategic objectives? We'll need to make sure everyone aligns his or her visual management meetings and process confirmation time. I'll send out an email and collect everyone's preferred diary standards and then I'll facilitate a small workshop where we agree it. I'll also talk to the IT department. I'm fairly sure they'll be able to tailor the standard diary online so that time is blocked out in all our online diaries.'

'Thanks, Paul,' said Sarah, 'I thought you might like the idea and your support is appreciated.'

They continued on together to review the short interval control management areas.

On the Tuesday of the third week, Paul walked over to his team's visual display to carry out the weekly process confirmation.

Safety and engineering were showing green status. Operations and customer services were both red. The visual display for operations showed that productivity and the lead KPIs for operations were all green, but that the liquidated damages KPI was red. This KPI had never achieved green status since being set up many weeks earlier. The customer services KPIs reflected the issue with liquidated damages: several customers were repeatedly claiming against contractual failures.

Paul stood back and checked the visual display for one, three, ten and standards adherence. Once he was satisfied, he quickly began to look at each chart and apply his initials and the date. He was happy that all charts were to standard and that the visual display was focused on the right things. Where there were red flags, he paused to consider whether he agreed with these being the main risks, based on his knowledge of current affairs and events. He considered actions and whether these gave him confidence in their ability to address the problems satisfactorily. He nodded and mumbled to himself that this was what he expected to see: no surprises and a good alignment with his own thinking.

Paul went back to the liquidated damages KPI to study it more closely. The target line was showing two per cent max and the various red crosses were plotting between three per cent and four per cent. To the right of the chart, Sarah had pinned up a Pareto chart to start to focus on causes of the problem. It showed the breakdown of liquidated damages by customer type and the largest bar was showing that contracts for hire services accounted for sixty-five per cent of all liquidated damages charges. Next to that chart was a second Pareto chart, a breakdown of the customer industries relating to hire service contracts. This chart's largest bar showed that seventy-five per cent of hire service liquidated damages came from nuclear industry clients. Paul made a quick calculation in his head: seventy-five per cent of sixty-five per cent was nearly fifty per cent. Therefore, solving the problem of hire service liquidated damages for nuclear clients would halve the current KPI and achieve the target. Paul made a note of this and decided that he would dig into this matter during the visual management meeting.

At 11 a.m. Sarah, Peter, Helen, Brian and their deputies stood around the visual display. After a short review of actions, the meeting moved onto the three minute presentations by each head of department. Safety was first and Brian came forward to present. He stood in front of his visual display and summarised his department's performance in thirty seconds.

Next up was Sarah. 'As you can see,' she said, 'operations is red again for this week. We only have one red KPI and this is for liquidated damages. The KPI was four per cent last week and this is double the target level. The main cause of liquidated damages is late delivery, even though our delivery performance is now very high on average. The consequence of failing to get this down to the target level is that we are losing profit through fines and this threatens our strategic objectives. The actions we have taken have been focused around putting more resources into certain areas of operations, and improved training, but this is not working. We have started to focus on the problem and create Pareto charts.'

She pointed to them.

'You can see the two Pareto charts we have produced to the right of the KPI chart. 'These charts show that the problem is predominantly due to late delivery of hire equipment to our nuclear sector customers. This includes power stations, reprocessing plants, decommissioning and fuel production plants. Due to the current growth of this industry we are supplying a lot of equipment on both hire and maintenance contracts. We mainly supply tower cranes and other large scale lifting devices.'

Paul nodded. 'What have our latest actions been to address this issue?'

'I've just hired additional expertise from consultants with industry-specific knowledge.'

'How confident are you that this will be effective?' asked Paul

'I believe it will be effective,' said Sarah, 'but very expensive.'

She walked over to a table and picked up a piece of paper. She pinned the paper onto the visual display to the right of the Pareto charts (refer to Figure 23).

PARETO CHART – SARAH (OPERATIONS)

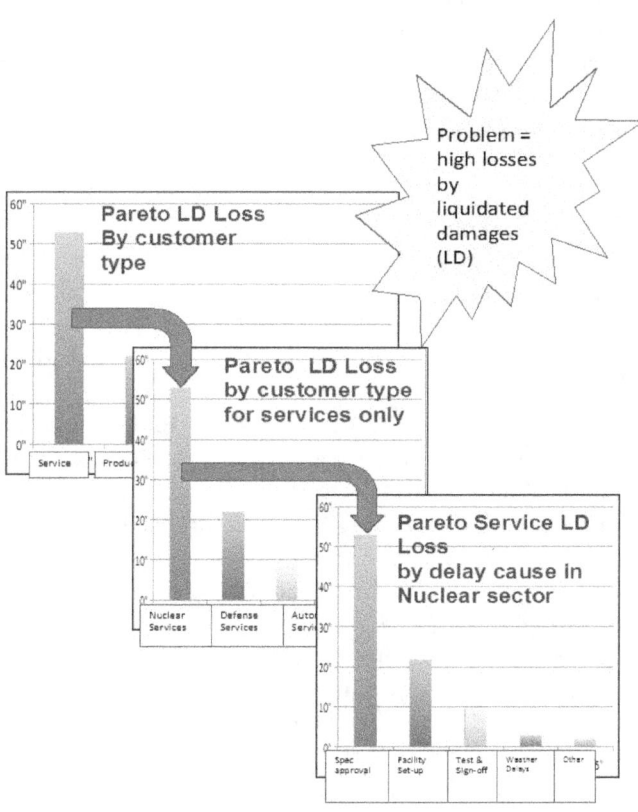

FIGURE 23

'This is my latest Pareto chart,' she said. 'As you can see, we've produced a chart to break down the delivery delays into the different areas of the hire process. The largest bar on this chart clearly shows that most time is lost during the approval process. Without approval, we cannot install the crane. The approval process requires the highest level of expertise to get it right and that's why I hired specialists.'

'Mmm,' said Paul. 'I'm not convinced we're getting to the root cause of this issue and this is now an urgent matter. I'd like you to gather your most knowledgeable people and produce a 5 Whys analysis on why the approvals are delayed. Do it today, please, and bring it to my office at 5 p.m.'

Sarah nodded. 'I'll do that.'

Paul recorded the action and the meeting moved on.

The remainder of the meeting progressed quickly and smoothly. Peter echoed Sarah's concerns about liquidated damages. He said he was containing the issue by spending more time with affected customers and also using his contacts to gather more in-depth knowledge around the specifics of the problem. Paul asked him to also attend the 5 p.m. meeting.

***

Just before five, Paul returned to his office after spending most of his afternoon out and about in the workplace. He found Sarah, Peter and four other people waiting for him.

Paul opened the door and ushered everyone in.

'Please take a seat,' he said, inviting everyone to sit around the meeting table.

'Please let me introduce David, Clive, Angela and Philip,' said Sarah.

Paul shook hands with each of them and then proceeded to set the scene.

'The liquidated damages KPI is continually above target. We are targeting two per cent maximum and achieving between three and four per cent week on week. I want to get to the root cause of the problem. The work you've done so far with Pareto analysis has gone a long way towards pinpointing where the main problem lies. If we can now solve the root cause issue of late delivery of hired equipment to the nuclear industry, then we'll achieve our target of two per cent. I believe you have a 5 Whys analysis to show me.'

David nodded and laid a folder on the table. He flipped it open and produced an A3 sheet of paper, which he passed to Paul.

'This shows our analysis,' he said.

Paul saw that it showed the three Pareto charts. Below the charts were listed the containment actions that were being taken, and below those was a diagram of the process flow from order receipt through to installation of the equipment on the client's site.

Angela pointed to the Pareto charts. 'As you can see, the biggest delays come from the customer approval process. This includes their approval of the specification and the safety case.'

Paul glanced at the process flow and noticed that specification approval and safety case were highlighted on the process flow diagram. The standard contractual time was six weeks from customer order to approval of the specification and the safety case.

'Could you explain what the safety case is?' asked Paul.

'A safety case,' said Clive, 'is a document that highlights all risks and hazards and also describes how we will control and mitigate them.'

'As we are installing a crane on a nuclear facility,' said Peter, 'there are big risks both during installation and operation of the crane.'

Paul nodded. 'I see.'

'We've broken down the process flow for the safety case approval,' said David. 'You can see it here.' He pointed to a detailed diagram.

'Okay,' said Paul. 'Before we start diving off into more detail, let's take a look at your 5 Whys analysis.'

David pointed to the 5 Whys analysis on the right hand side of the page and Paul took some time to read through it (refer to Figure 24).

Paul studied the analysis carefully.

'How often do our safety cases get rejected?' he asked.

Sarah sighed. 'So far, every one of our first off submissions has been rejected. About fifty per cent of our second attempts are rejected, too.'

Paul was shocked. 'So that means we lose a minimum of two weeks on every contract,' he said, 'and on fifty per cent of them we lose at least four weeks. I'm guessing that our quotation is based on first time acceptance?'

Peter nodded. 'That's correct,' he said, 'and it's what the customer expects.'

'Okay,' said Paul. 'So if we're going to solve this problem then we could either reduce the reapproval time or find a way to ensure we get a right first time submission.'

Everyone nodded.

Paul paused for thought and sat silently for a couple of minutes looking at the 5 Whys analysis. 'I don't think we have quite finished the 5 Whys analysis,' he said.

Everyone looked up expectantly.

'Why do we not have access to the approval panel people?' Paul asked. 'I believe this is the key. We need support from the right people to build quality into the safety case and achieve first time approval.'

5 WHYS ANALYSIS

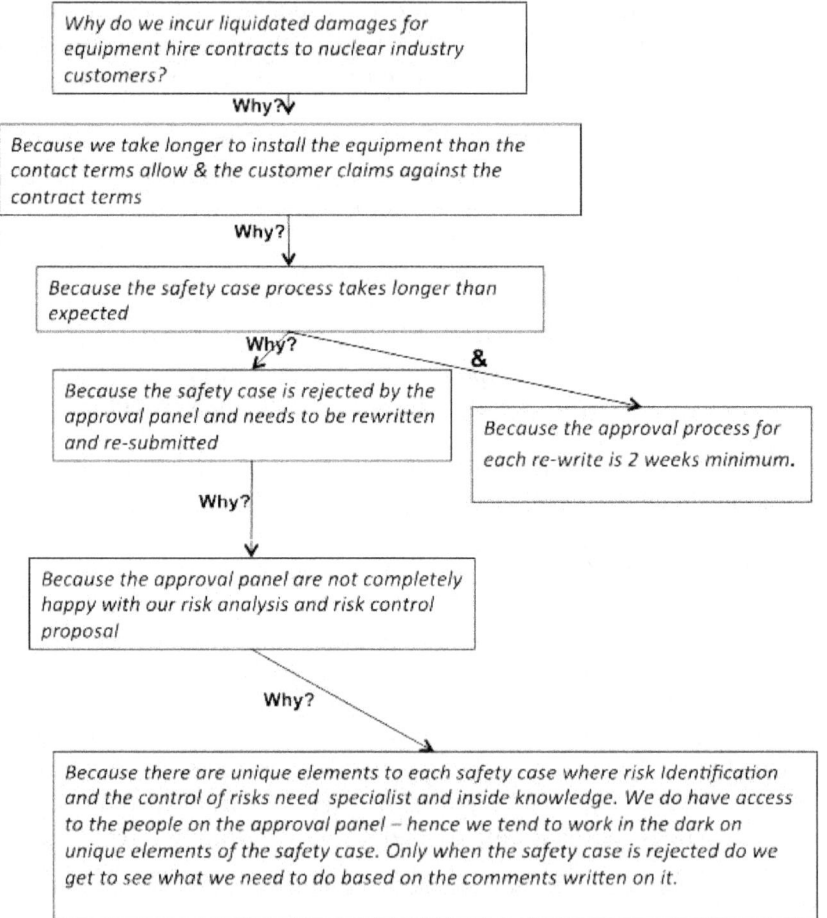

FIGURE 24

'They don't want to deal with us,' said Philip. 'I tried to contact them but I was told that their names could not be given out and that I must stick to the process.'

'Peter, as you are closest to the customer, could you do some digging and make some phone calls for us?' asked Sarah

'Yes, of course,' said Peter.

'Could you find out who these approval people are? Could you also talk to your commercial contacts at the customer and explain the problem to them. Surely the customer wants the crane to be installed on time rather than claiming against penalty clauses in the contract. Maybe they can help us get access to the right people.'

'Okay,' said Peter. 'Can you give me an hour?'

'Fine,' said Paul. 'I propose we take a break and come back in one hour.'

***

One hour later the team reassembled in Paul's office.

'Peter, what have you found out?' asked Paul.

'I had to do a lot of phoning around,' said Peter, 'but I found out quite a lot of information. Firstly I found out that the two week delay is because the safety case approval board is scheduled every two weeks as a half-day meeting. They review lots of safety cases during this half-day. A safety case needs unanimous approval from the approval panel to be sanctioned. Therefore, all the relevant people need to come together and they don't all work on one site. I was told there's little chance that we can get them to come together just to review our resubmission, so that idea is out. I also tried to find out who the review panel people are. I found out the name of one of them from my commercial contact and I tracked him down. He said he didn't have the time to spare for external contractors like us, but he did give me the name of a lady that used to be on the safety case approval board. He said that she is highly respected, well known by most nuclear approval boards, and that having her name on the safety case documents would go a long way towards increasing confidence that our safety case was sound. She recently retired, but is available for part-time freelance work. I got her phone number and after speaking to her she said she'd like to work for us on a freelance basis.'

'That's great news,' said Sarah.

'Here are her contact details,' said Peter. 'He handed over a slip of paper with a name and phone number on it.

***

After another three weeks, the liquidated damages KPI hit green for the first time. Paul finally started to feel a little more relaxed; he was beginning to enjoy the process of being a manager.

In addition to the green KPIs, the project to implement the new computer system was now on track. The project had started to slip and Paul had worked on a 5 Whys analysis with his team to understand what was going wrong. At the root of the problem was the lack of liaison between the various stakeholders, and their failure to proactively plan detailed activities based on the day-to-day reality of the project. Paul's team all agreed to push the computer project from a weekly review to a daily review, with the full involvement of all contractors, electricians, IT people and reps from all departments (refer to Figures 25a and 25b).

VISUAL PROJECT MANAGEMENT EXAMPLE 1

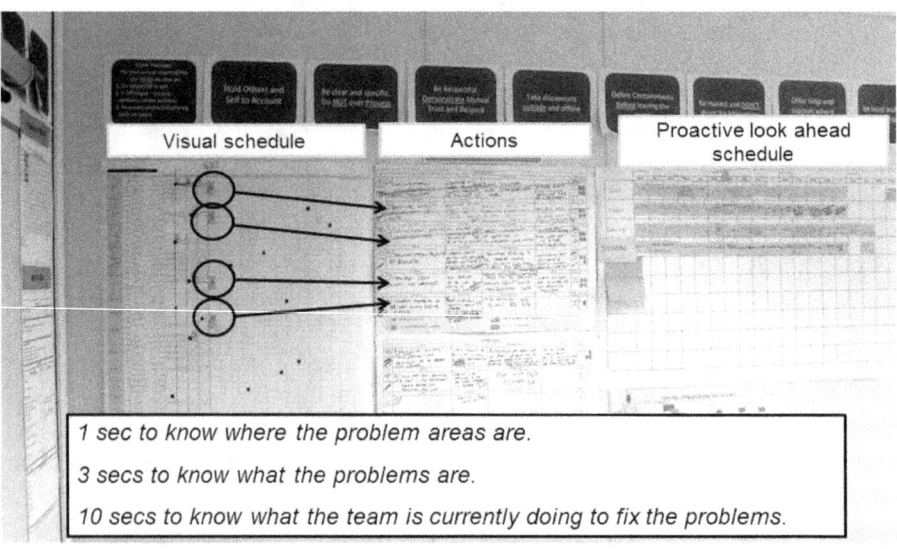

FIGURE 25a

VISUAL PROJECT MANAGEMENT EXAMPLE 2

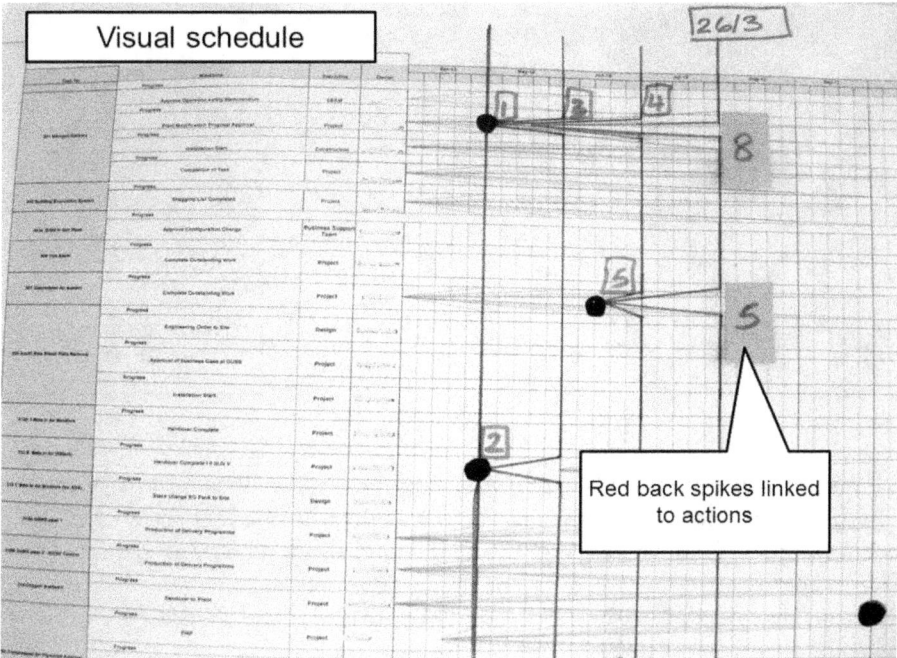

FIGURE 25b

These people reviewed plans at the start of each day and produced a rolling three-week look-ahead plan that showed detailed deliverables for every person at the meeting (refer to Figure 26).

VISUAL PROJECT MANAGEMENT EXAMPLE 3

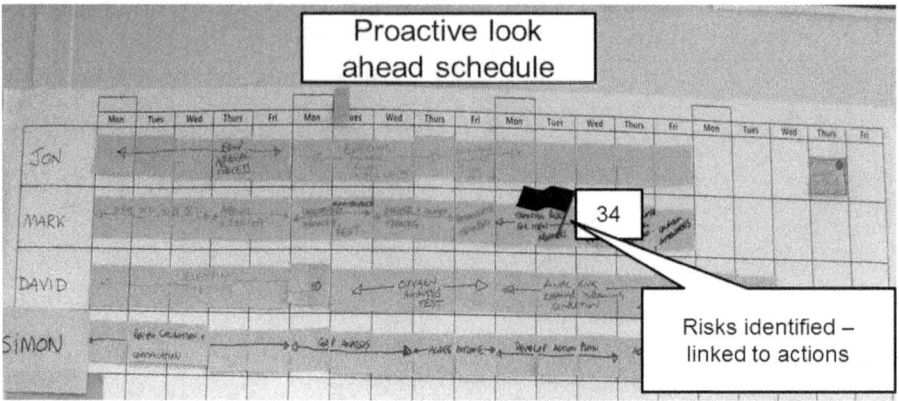

FIGURE 26

This look-ahead plan was visually displayed on the wall using Post-it notes. The plan was updated daily using a green highlighter pen to show what had been completed and a red highlighter pen to show what was behind. Red flags were also used to show where up and coming tasks were at risk due to an issue that needed to be resolved. This proved to be an effective way of bringing the project back on track.

On the Friday of the sixth week, Paul had just finished attending a lower level daily visual management meeting when he received a call on his mobile phone.

'Hi, Paul, this is Ed. I'd like to talk to you. Could you please come to my office?'

'Yes, of course,' said Paul. 'Do you want me to come right now?'

'Yes, please,' said Ed. 'See you shortly.' He put down the phone.

Paul headed immediately to Ed's office. When he arrived, he knocked on Ed's door and was invited in by the now familiar voice.

Paul walked in and found Ed standing. They shook hands.

'Take a seat,' said Ed. Paul did so, and Ed sat behind his desk.

'I want to congratulate you, Paul. The results you are now achieving are good. I had my doubts about you and in my mind your chances of making it in this company were fifty-fifty. You've done a great job and really grown as a manager. Did you enjoy the process?'

Paul wasn't sure what to say. He wanted to say, *No, I was really worried about losing my job.*

'I feel good about it now,' he said, 'but there were times when I was unsure of myself. The challenge you set was really tough: there were days when I felt stressed out and I doubted myself and my abilities. I'm glad I came through it.'

Ed smiled. 'When you think back to your childhood, can you remember the names of the people that really pushed you to achieve something you were proud of? Maybe this was in sport or at school or a hobby. I bet you can remember the names of those people. Equally, I bet you can't remember the names of the people who let you off easily and allowed to underachieve, can you?'

'That's true,' said Paul. 'I can remember a few notable people and you're right, they're people that helped me achieve the things I'm proud of.'

'The fact is,' said Ed, 'if I hadn't challenged you, but had simply left you to continue as you were, you would have lost your job and so would all the people that work for you. Did you realise that?'

'Really?' said Paul, surprised by this new revelation.

Ed looked Paul in the eyes and nodded his head slowly. 'We bought your company for peanuts,' he said. 'We do our best to give our acquisitions a chance, but we always know we can make money by breaking companies up and selling them off in bits if we need to. A sad fact, and I prefer not to work that way. At least my company gives people a chance; many don't in my line of business.

'I need to ask you another question, Paul. As you know, I set some strategic targets. You and your team are now achieving those targets. Many parts of the organisation, however, are not achieving them. What would you do to improve that situation if you were me?'

'Based on what I've learned,' said Paul, 'the first thing I would do is go and look to see what is really going on. I would want to understand the reality of the situation, what the results currently look like, how the systems work, what activities underpin the results, where the problems are and what actions are currently being taken to improve the situation. If the status of results and activities are not visible, then I would start by creating that visibility. I would challenge, coach and support people to focus on results, solve problems, set standards and create solutions that address the root causes.' Paul surprised himself with the clarity of his answer.

Ed continued to look Paul squarely in the eyes. 'I want you to go and do exactly that.'

'What do you mean?'

'I'm moving on, Paul. I need to move on to the next company we are taking over that's not making any money. I'm recommending you for promotion to the position of Director of Operations for the entire organisation. I want you to go and do exactly what you just described to me and get results. Do you think you can do that?'

'I'm certainly willing to give it a try,' said Paul.

'Good. I leave at the end of the month and you'll need to consider a successor of your own.'

'Thank you, Ed. I really mean it.'

'Do not disappoint me,' said Ed. He smiled briefly. 'Lastly, Paul, You are due for your monthly meeting with me and I need to do some coaching with you.'

'Okay,' said Paul. 'I'm ready for anything right now.'

'I have a problem with your KPIs,' said Ed.

'But I thought you just said we had done a good job,' said Paul. 'What's wrong with my KPIs?'

'They're all green,' said Ed. 'I want you to make some of them go red.'

'I'm sorry?' said Paul, assuming he had misheard.

'Do you remember turning the triangle upside down?'

Paul nodded. 'Of course,' he said. 'Challenge, coach and support.'

'Exactly. The problem once all the KPIs go green is that the challenge starts to disappear and people will drop back into their comfort zones. You need to find a new way to keep up the challenge.'

'How do I do that?'

'There are various methods. You could increase the targets. You could change people around. You could increase the level of training. You could refuse to replace a person that resigns. You could take on more business. You could run more improvement workshops. I'm sure if you think about it you'll find a way. I can see by your face that you feel uncomfortable about this, and that's good.

'Good luck, Paul. I'll still visit and coach you once per month and I'll still come over to carry out process confirmation, but starting from the end of next week, I want to hand over the reins to you.'

Ed put out his hand and Paul shook it warmly.

Chapter 12

Looking to the future

Back in his office, Paul had one last thing to do before he headed home. He picked up the phone and tapped in Mike's number.

'Mike? Paul Wayman. How are you?'

'Hey, Paul, good to hear from you,' Mike said. 'I'm great, thanks. Thinking about summer holidays and wondering where to go. How are things going with you?'

'Very well indeed, thanks in no small part to you. I just wanted to say thank you for all the help you've given me over the last few months.'

'Oh, you're welcome. I just did for you what someone did for me when I was in your position. All I ask is that when the time comes, you pass it all on and help someone else.'

'You can count on it. In fact, that might be necessary sooner rather than later. I've just heard from Ed that he's moving on.'

'That usually seems to be the sign they're looking at another acquisition,' said Mike. 'Has he said anything about who'll be replacing him?'

'Actually, he's recommended me as his replacement.'

'I was hoping you'd say that, that's great news. You've earned it, Paul. You've made huge strides over the last few months.'

'It's been a steep learning curve, that's for sure.'

'But you did it! How many of your colleagues worked as hard as you to get to grips with the new way of working?'

Paul reflected. Of the original management team, just half were currently still in post, and none had as yet been promoted. 'Not many,' he said.

'And now that you've got to grips with it, how much easier is your job going to be?'

'Oh, it's been a revelation, and a revolution! Focusing on facts, recognising that processes cause problems and getting away from blaming people, with all the strain and upset involved in that, pre-empting problems and stopping them from happening, sorting things out calmly and methodically ... I can't believe how much time and energy we all wasted, and how little we really knew about what was going on.'

'Yes, that's pretty much how I felt when I got to grips with it all,' said Mike. 'Anyway, congratulations on your promotion, it's well deserved!'

'I haven't got it yet, it's just a recommendation.'

'I think it would be very unlikely if it were to fall through. Ring me when it's all confirmed.'

Paul laughed. 'Okay, Mike will do. Thanks again for everything!'

Paul grabbed his jacket and his satchel and headed for the car.

He made a detour on the way home, stopping at the huge shopping centre on the outskirts of the town. He had just two ports of call and was soon hurrying back to the car with a bottle of Rebecca's favourite perfume and a huge basket of flowers – he had some making up to do. It was time he came clean about the problems he'd been having at work and how that had affected his mood. Time to tell her that he'd overcome them, and was in line for a promotion, too. He figured that was a conversation to have over dinner in their favourite restaurant.

As he drove, he reflected on the changes of the last few months. He'd been catapulted out of his comfort zone and learned so much, so quickly. He'd been made to realise how much of a rut he'd been in – he and his team had just been going through the motions, doing the same old things in the same old way, day after day. He thought of the huge monthly reports they'd produced, too unwieldy to be of any use in steering the business, lying unread in a filing cabinet – but a box ticked because they'd been produced. How many things had he done over the years that made absolutely no difference whatsoever?

Now he really felt as though he had a handle on things. He understood what his team did. He knew the problems they coped with. He knew – and so did they – how to cope with both chronic and acute problems when they cropped up, and also how to tell the difference between them. There would be no more sweeping issues under the rug and pretending everything was fine if it wasn't, no more finger-pointing and angry attempts to shift the blame when something blew up and caused a problem. It felt like a much better way of working, more worthwhile, more satisfying.

He parked up outside the house and rang the restaurant to book a table before he went inside.

'In the kitchen!' shouted Rebecca, when she heard the front door, then 'What's all this? Paul?' when he appeared, laden down with flowers and clutching a Jo Malone bag.

'For you. I'm sorry I've been such a pain lately.'

'Oh, thank you,' she said, taking the flowers from him and putting them down on the table. 'These are so beautiful. And perfume, too!'

'I've booked us a table for dinner, as well,' he said. 'It's time to celebrate.'

'It is,' said Rebecca. 'Mum's got the all clear after her hip operation. She can move into the nursing home this weekend.'

'That's fantastic, great news! That'll make life easier.'

'I owe you an apology, too.' said Rebecca. 'I've been so stressed about Mum, and missing the girls, I know I've been on a short fuse—'

'Don't worry about it. I've got lots to tell you, but let's make this a new start for us all, eh?'

***

Later, over dinner, Paul had described the problems he'd been facing at work.

'So you're telling me that over the course of nine weeks, you went from fearing you'd be out of a job to knowing you were in line for a huge promotion?' Rebecca said.

'That's about the size of it,' said Paul. 'And do you know what? I really feel like I've earned it, not just been given it because of some arbitrary reason, like it's my turn or there's no one else to give it to.'

'How does that feel?'

Fantastic!' he said, and he raised his glass. 'Here's to us, and to the future.'

'To us, and to the future,' said Rebecca, and they drank their toast.

'I have a good feeling about things now,' said Paul. 'I really think we're going to be fine.'

'It'll be nice to get a chance to catch our breath.'

'That's for sure.' But for all he said that, Paul had no intention of standing still. He couldn't wait to see how far visual management could take him, his team, and the business; for the first time in years he was genuinely excited about work!

JON MORETON

Appendices

1. Key Performance Indicators (KPIs)

A key performance indicator, or KPI for short, is a measurable value that demonstrates how effectively a key business objective is being achieved. For example, the top business KPIs for many companies are profit, return on investment, and cash flow. Each of these can be tracked on a yearly, monthly, weekly, or even daily basis. We can apply targets to each of these. For example, we could set a target of ten per cent minimum for profit and track this weekly. If the company makes ten per cent or more, then we say it is on target and gets a green 'O', but if it makes less than ten per cent then it is off target and gets a red 'X'. Directors often also set top-level objectives each year that set the direction to both perform and improve. Each department must directly or indirectly contribute to these top-level KPIs and objectives.

At a departmental level it is often tricky to use top-level KPIs because they may not very well lend themselves to the daily operations of the department. The challenge is working out the most relevant and important KPIs for the department that contribute to the top-level KPIs and objectives.

Managers have a responsibility to make sure their teams focus on delivering the right results and at the same time use the right activities to achieve those results. There is a famous story from India where the government wanted to reduce the number of poisonous snakes in Delhi. Their result KPI was the number of poisonous snakes on the loose in Delhi with a target to reduce this number. To drive improvement of this top level KPI, they decided to track the number of cobras killed on a daily basis: more dead cobras equalled less live cobras on the loose. The government started to offer a cash reward for each dead cobra evidenced. Unfortunately this led to people breeding large numbers of cobras so that they could then kill them and earn money. The number of cobras in the wild actually increased instead of decreasing. This phenomenon has become known as the cobra effect and this is why managers need to be very hands-on with their teams to select the right KPIs, and activities to achieve the KPIs.

2. Pareto charts (as used for problem-solving against KPI charts)

A Pareto chart is simply an ordered bar chart, where the bars are put in order starting with the largest one first. Pareto charts are named after Vilfredo Pareto, a nineteenth century Italian economist. Pareto observed that 80% of the income in Italy went to 20% of the population. He also carried out surveys on other countries and found that their income distribution was the same – 80% of the income to 20% of the population.

The 80/20 rule appears to apply to almost anything:

- 80% of profits come from 20% of customers.
- 80% of delays result from 20% of the possible causes of the delays.
- 80% of customer complaints arise from 20% of your services.
- 80% of your company revenues come from 20% of your sales force.
- 80% of system problems are due to 20% of the possible causes.

The benefit of the Pareto chart is that it shows us the vital few issues we need to resolve to greatly improve performance. We can use Pareto charts to first of all direct us to the area where the problem is most prominent and then create a second or third Pareto to focus on the causes in this area. This enables us to direct resources to the most important areas and solve those problems that will have the biggest impact.

Pareto charts show the vital few problems in order of significance. The largest bar represents the problem or area that has contributed the most to the negative effect.

When a Pareto chart is first started, the order of the problems changes several times over a number of weeks, but over time a trend develops whereby a small number of repeating problems begin to dominate. This is because these problems are built into the process and will repeat over time. The vital few problems stay as the vital few problems until they are solved.

Pareto charts can be scaled by cost or by count. If possible, Pareto charts should be scaled by cost, because cost is generally of greater importance to the business.

Care should be taken with flat Paretos. (Refer to Figure 27.)

FLAT PARETO CHARTS

If we gather data in the wrong way we can end up with flat Pareto charts. By separating the data of a major problem into too many problem areas we can end up with many bars with little data in each of them. This will create a flat Pareto chart. By re-grouping the problems we can show a true Pareto chart (see Figure 28). We are looking for one root cause responsible for the problem group.

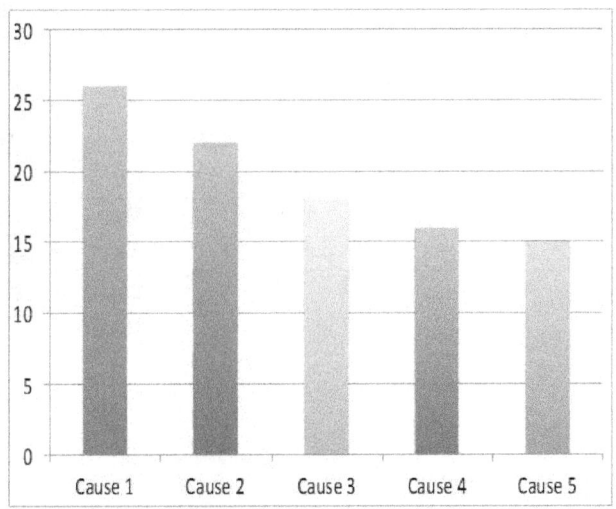

FIGURE 27

A good Pareto chart will show the top three categories accounting for a minimum 80% of the cost (or number of incidents) and the first category accounting for at least 50% of the cost (or number of incidents). A good Pareto chart means that a small number of root causes are driving a large part of the problem. Solving these root causes will have a big impact. A flat Pareto may mean that a large number of root causes are driving many problems (refer to Figure 27). Alternatively, a flat Pareto may mean that we have not collected data for long enough or that we have broken down a problem, with a single root cause, into too many categories (refer to Figure 28).

FLAT PARETO CHART

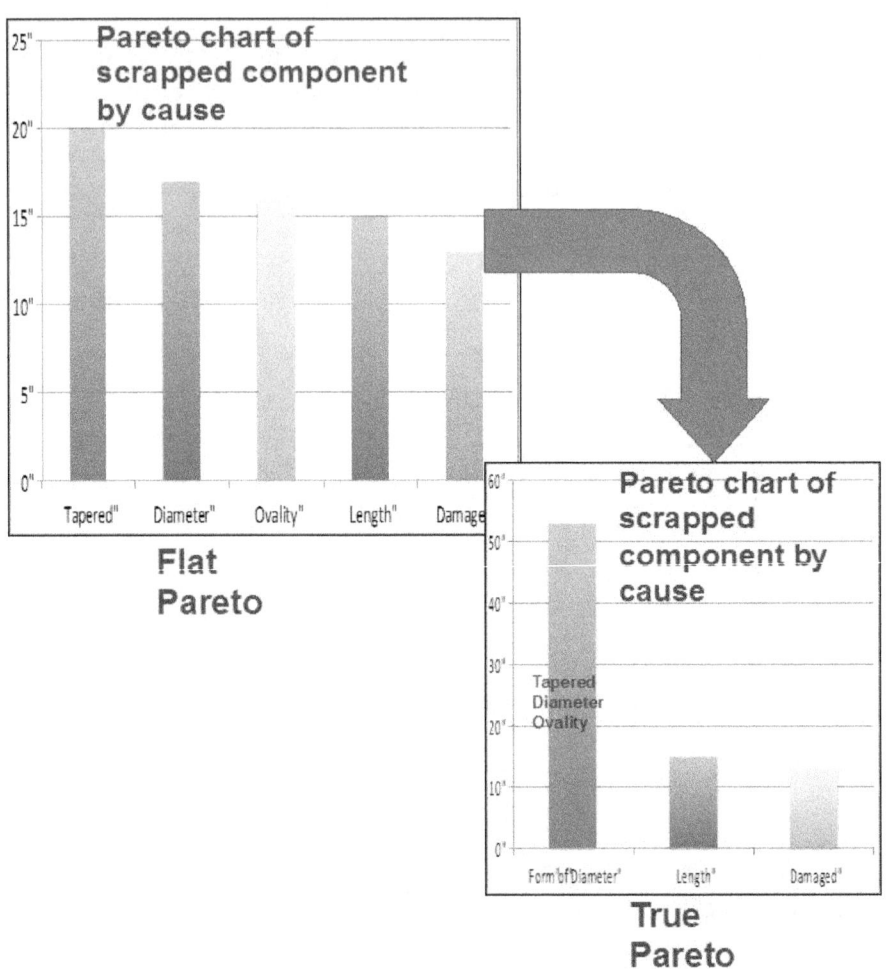

FIGURE 28

3. Acute and chronic problems

Acute problems tend to be sudden and unexpected. They can be severe, but are often one off events. If you fall out of a tree and break your arm, then that is an acute problem.

Chronic problems are ongoing problems that may develop over a long time. Osteoporosis is an example of a chronic problem and may lead to a broken bone.

If you were considering buying a house and at one time the house had been flooded due to a flash flood, that would be an acute problem. If, on the other hand, the flooding was due to the house being in a flood plain, then that would be a chronic problem. Chronic problems will cause repeated effects. Chronic problems are built into the process or the system.

4. Root cause analysis

Root cause analysis is a method used to get to the root of a problem so that a permanent fix (called a countermeasure) can be applied. Quick actions to fix a problem are often only containments. If you have an infection then taking painkillers may take away the symptoms, but it will not cure the problem. The painkillers are merely a containment action. Root cause analysis answers the question, why did this problem occur in the first place?

There is no one agreed upon definition for the term 'root cause', but a useful definition is that a root cause is the lowest level cause (or causes) that can be practically fixed to prevent the problem from reccurring.

A simple method you can use to dig down to the root cause is '5 Whys analysis'. By asking 'why?' multiple times, we can dig down to the root of the problem. Although the technique is called 5 Whys it may take as little 3 whys or as many as 10 whys to get to the root of the problem.

5 Whys example

I am in pain – immediate containment = take some painkillers.
Why am I in pain?
Because I broke my arm – fix the broken bone.
Why did I break my arm?
Because I fell down the stairs.
Why did I fall down the stairs?
Because I tripped over.
Why did I trip over?
Because a step was broken – fix the broken step.

Why was the step broken?
Because it was rotten.
Why was it rotten?
Because the paint had worn out and the moisture got in.
Why?
Because it was not checked and maintained – check and maintain all steps.
Why?
Because there is no schedule for checking and maintaining the safety of infrastructure assets. Countermeasure = put a schedule in place to check and maintain the safety of all infrastructure assets.

N.B. There is more information on the 5 Whys technique below.

5. Turning the triangle upside down

The typical organisation diagram looks like a triangle. The CEO is at the very top, the managers in the middle, and an army of front line people are at the bottom. The leadership style traditionally adopted with this model is one of management direction from above. Directors and managers are typically responsible for telling people what to do and for solving business problems. Consequently, a minority of people carry out the thinking and problem-solving. The majority is responsible for following instructions and can easily become disengaged.

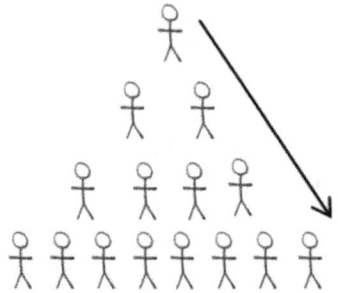

Turning the triangle upside down puts the front line people at the top. Managers and directors take on the role of challenging, coaching and supporting from below. This model puts the front line people at the top because they are closest to where the value is added and closest to the customer. They are, therefore, often in the best position to solve problems and determine workable solutions. This results in a higher level of employee engagement, employee development, motivation and improvement.

The danger is that this model can be misinterpreted as a hands-off style of management involvement. Managers can easily abdicate their responsibility in the name of trust and delegation. Without challenge, people may not feel the need to solve problems and improve. Without coaching, people may not develop their abilities to meet the challenges. Without support, people may feel abandoned when they meet obstacles they cannot come overcome at their level within the organisation.

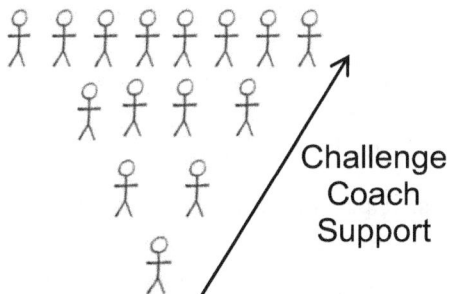

6. Management coaching

'Coaching is a management behaviour that lies at the opposite end of the spectrum to command and control.' – John Whitmore, *Coaching for Performance*.

The benefit of coaching is that it develops people to solve their own problems and creates a higher level of motivation.

At the heart of effective coaching is the skill of asking questions rather than giving answers. Questions can be used to help people think through a problem for themselves. Questions can help people identify their options, evaluate blind spots in their thinking and pin down their commitment to action. As John Whitmore says, 'Coaching is about building awareness, responsibility and self-belief.'

Other coaching skills include listening, giving feedback, playing back what someone has said, and following up on commitments made. Offering suggestions is usually reserved for when the coachee asks for them or when the coachee is inexperienced in a particular area.

A coaching style of management does not absolve managers from the responsibility to use direction when the situation demands it – usually when speed of execution is of high importance.

Managers also have a responsibility to ensure that standards are maintained and this often requires a combination of feedback and direction.

7. Flag and follow up

A simple technique where a leader consistently follows up when she asks for something to be done or receives a commitment from someone. Leading by example also requires the leader to apply flag and follow up to themselves; they must always do what they say they will do. The technique requires simple handwritten notes to be kept from coaching sessions and discussions. There are positive benefits from flag and follow up because following up with people allows the leader many opportunities to give praise.

8. Visual Management benefits

- Builds team participation through shared information.
- Visually exposes problems.
- Motivates everyone to improve by clarifying performance targets.
- Enables a team to see each other's challenges and how they support each other – i.e. how their targets interconnect and are interdependent.
- Makes the status of the business easier to understand.
- Makes operational standards quicker to understand.
- Creates status visibility for all stakeholders.
- Creates clear accountability.
- Captures and drives action to improve.
- Ensures problems and risks are dealt with promptly.
- Drives the escalation of problems.
- Enables interdependencies to be seen and understood.

9. Lead and lag KPIs

Lag KPIs are results indicators and measure the output. They tell us how the company or system has performed in the past. They are generally easy to measure, but they are reactive measures because improvement action is taken to improve by reacting to the result they show. They also give no indication as to what future results might look like.

Lead KPIs are input and process indicators and tell us how the company or system is performing. They measure the inputs and the processes that create the output result. Leading KPIs are predictive of the lag KPIs because if the lead KPIs are going in the right direction we can predict that the lag KPIs will also go in the right direction.

Lead KPIs are often measured more frequently than lag KPIs so that timely action can be taken to ensure they move in the right direction. Lead KPIs can be both reactive and proactive.

A special form of leading KPI is the activity KPI. These are proactive KPIs that measure activities designed to positively influence both lead and lag KPIs. Skills development, training, auditing activities, process design, and improvement workshops are all examples of proactive activities.

Example:

Body weight = Lag KPI (reactive)
Calorie intake = Lead KPI (reactive)
Calories burned = Lead KPI (reactive)
Exercise schedule = Lead Activity KPI (proactive)

10. Process confirmation

Process confirmation is an activity undertaken by all levels of management to confirm that activities are being carried out to the correct standard at the right time and frequency and are giving the expected results. The technique is used in conjunction with a coaching style of management to guide people back to the correct standard by identifying deviations from standard quickly. This cannot be achieved from within an office and requires managers to go out into the workplace.

Process confirmation can be used for all standardised activities within the workplace, not just for visual management and is often carried out to a schedule. Skip level process confirmation means that managers skip over the level of manager below them and carry out process confirmation at a lower level.

11. The KPI tree

The KPI tree is a graphical method of arranging KPIs that has two main purposes.
1. To clarify the links between lead and lag KPIs to ensure the right things are measured (and actioned) at the right place, at the right frequency and organisational level.

2. To clarify the responsibility at each level of the organisation for the achievement of both results and activities.

The KPI tree helps visualisation of how strategic objectives are turned into operational objectives and defined as measurable KPIs. The KPI tree is a useful tool to help teams of people work together to define their operational strategy and targets.

12. Performance improvement projects

A method of driving improvements by taking time out with selected staff to sit down and discuss ideas for improvement openly – identify potential improvements, try them out immediately or plan for their implementation. Step changes in improvement sometimes need people to be taken out of their busy daily routines to generate, agree and action ideas. Improvement experts can help run workshops and facilitate the process. Techniques such as process mapping can be helpful to visualise the current process, identify waste and create a picture of improved process.

13. Short interval control

A method used to drive many small process improvements during the day or shift. Short interval control is focused on front-line, lead KPIs. Process output results are recorded on an hourly basis. Managers and supervisors go to the process at defined intervals during the day or shift (e.g. every three hours) and observe the results. If the results are off target then quick actions are taken to correct course and implement small-scale rapid fixes. These actions result in performance improvement and help change organisational habits by instituting a high visibility hands on management approach to removing frustrating obstacles and hassles.

Management can also apply short interval control as a temporary measure when a particular area of the business starts to experience problems. By increasing the frequency of measurement, review and action, problems can often by solved and brought under control.

Short interval control is also used during visual management reviews where a leader decides that a problem is serious enough to warrant immediate action and follow-up: a leader may request an immediate action together with an hourly or bi-daily update on progress and results. (Refer to Figures 29a and 29b.)

SHORT INTERVAL CONTROL VISUAL DISPLAY

Time	Target	Actual	Problem and action
8AM	10 / 10	10 / 10	No Problems
9	10 / 20	5 / 15	Process running slow. Action - immediate call to maintenance
10	10 / 30	10 / 25	No Problems
11	10 / 40	5 / 30	Information missing. Action - Escalation to operations manager to find info
12	10 / 50	10 / 40	Action - organise overtime to catch back 1 hour of missed target
1PM	5 / 55		
2	10 / 65		
3	10 / 75		
4	10 / 85		
5	10 / 95		

FIGURE 29a

SHORT INTERVAL CONTROL VISUAL DISPLAY – DETAIL

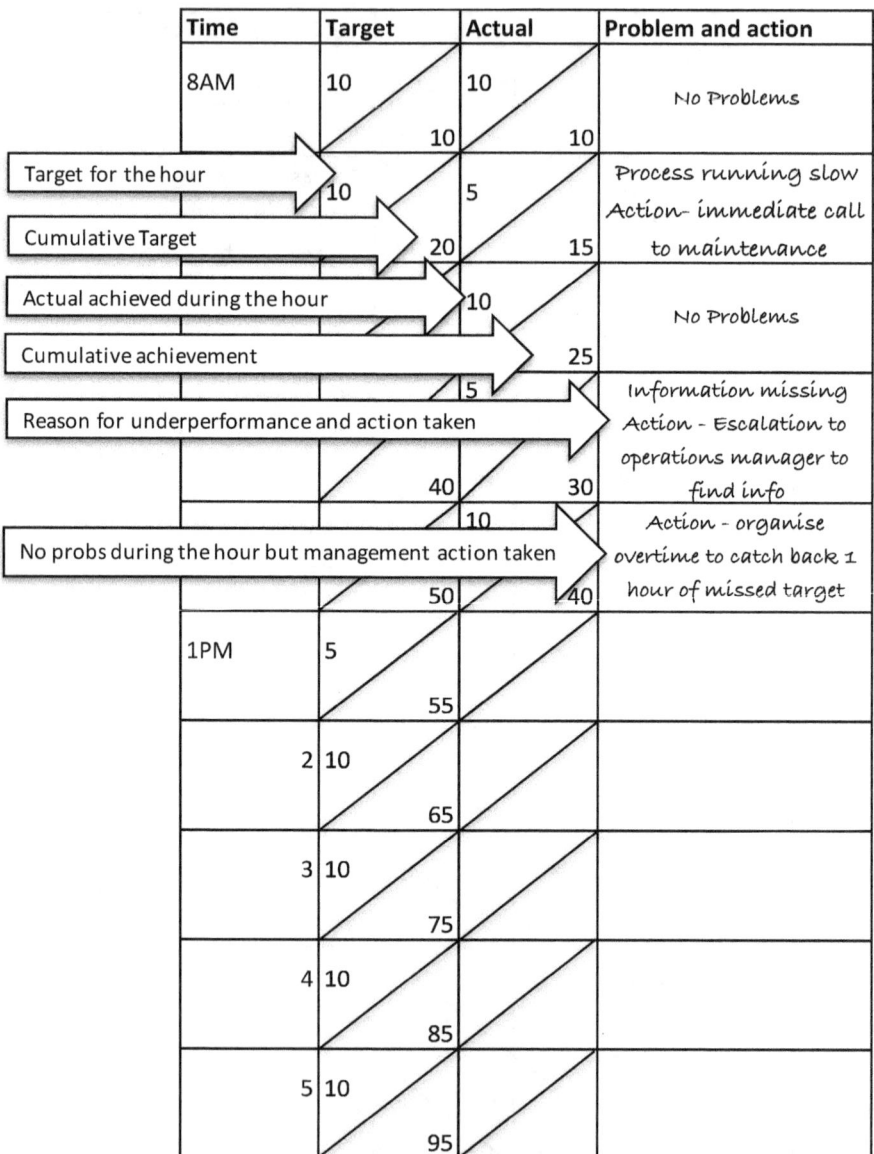

FIGURE 29b

14. 5 Whys analysis

A simple but powerful technique, 5 Whys is a problem-solving technique that allows you to get to the root cause of a problem fairly quickly. At the root of every technical problem there is a process problem. The goal of the 5 Whys is to help us see and coach others that chronic problems are caused by a bad process, not by bad people, and remedy the problem accordingly.

By repeatedly asking the question 'why?' (five times is a good rule), you can peel away the layers of symptoms that can lead to the root cause of a problem. Very often the first reason for a problem will lead you to another question and then to another.

Although this technique is called '5 Whys', you may find that you need to ask the questions fewer or more times than five before you find the issue / ultimate root cause related to a problem.

When to use 5 Whys analysis

- When it is important to get to root cause and avoid a work-around or sticking-plaster approach to solving the problem.
- When a mistake has been made – be tolerant of mistakes the first time they are made, but use 5 Whys to make sure the same mistake is never made again. Mistakes do happen and quick fix solutions are sometimes necessary, but you must put in processes to stop these becoming institutionalised behaviour.
- After a cause and effect (fishbone) diagram exercise to validate the root cause.

Examples

Why is the building project behind plan?

Because the contractors are delaying each other – *quick fix, intervene, bring them together and manage the interface.*

Why? – Because they both planned to use the same equipment at the same time.

Why? – Because they do not share plans or plan the next two weeks together.

Why? – Because they have no regular forum to share plans and see conflicts.

Why? – A joint planning meeting has not been set up and scheduled.

Why? – Not assumed to be necessary.

Solution – Set up a scheduled meeting and ensure joint planning for all contractor interfaces.

Why did the pump break?

Because the fuse has blown – quick fix is to replace the fuse.
  Why? – The motor is overloaded.
  Why? – The bearings are not lubricated correctly.
  Why? – The oil is contaminated.
  Why – The filter has not been cleaned regularly enough.
  Solution – Set up a process for cleaning the filter on a scheduled basis.

A solution can be applied at any point in the 5 Whys analysis – not just at the bottom.

Most problems that at first appear to be individual mistakes can often be traced back to one or more of the following:

1. 1. A poorly defined process or the lack of a process (e.g. no schedule for the filter).
2. 2. The lack of a set standard (e.g. the standard for a clean filter is not defined).
3. 3. Training has not been carried out or confirmed (assuming a defined standard and process).

15. The Hawthorne effect

The Hawthorne effect refers to the fact that people tend to change their behaviour when being observed. Studies have shown that human performance is enhanced due to increased attention. Increased attention by managers, customers or colleagues can bring about this result.

The Hawthorne effect gets its name from studies carried out during the 1920s in the Western Electric Company's Hawthorne Works. These studies were set up to test changes in working conditions and to identify their effects on productivity. The researchers found that all changes tended to result in increased productivity, including those that were perceived to worsen working conditions. The researchers were forced to conclude that the changes had nothing to do with the increases in productivity.

In 1939, Fritz J. Roethlisberger of Harvard Business School published a book called *Management and the Worker*, based on the studies at the Western Electric Company's Hawthorne Works. Fritz J. Roethlisberger concluded that financial incentives and working conditions were less important than previously thought. He proposed that important factors contributing towards human behaviour included the interest managers paid to their team, working as a group and treating people as valued members of the company.

Michel Anteby and Rakesh Khurana, both Professors of Harvard Business School, wrote an essay about the Hawthorne Studies titled, *A New Vision*:

'A manager's effectiveness, therefore, could be measured on the extent to which those in the organization internalized a common purpose and perceived the connection between their actions and the organization's ability to fulfil this common purpose. Management, then, was not about controlling human behaviour but unleashing human possibility.'

16. Standard diary

A method for protecting the time of important activities. A standard diary has blocks of time protected during the day to ensure that staff has time to carry out critical activities to support front line operations. No meetings or other activities can be booked during the protected blocks of time. Standard diaries create a form of standardised process for supervision and management by identifying those activities that need to be carried out and when they need to be carried out. Typical activities include process confirmation, shift start up support, checks, briefings, visual management meetings, management walk about.

JON MORETON

About the author

Jon Moreton is an operations improvement consultant. His more than 20 years' experience as an operations professional includes coaching management and employee teams in visual management, lean leadership, performance improvement and change management.

Jon has implemented visual management systems at leading international companies in industries as diverse as manufacturing, nuclear operations, construction, security services, defence and public transport. The main focus of his consulting practice is the delivery of enhanced results through the improvement of operations management.

Originally trained as an automotive engineer, Jon progressed into engineering management and the transformation of inefficient manufacturing plants. For the past ten years he has operated mainly outside of the manufacturing sector.

Jon can be contacted at jon@jdml.co.uk.

www.ingramcontent.com/pod-product-compliance
Lightning Source LLC
Chambersburg PA
CBHW060854170526
45158CB00001B/346